An Indian Face
of the Christian Faith

(Dharma Bharathi Darsana Samhita)

An Indian Face of the Christian Faith

(Dharma Bharathi Darsana Samhita)

Acharyasri

2022

An Indian Face of the Christian Faith (Dharma Bharathi Darsana Samhita)- published by the Indian Society for Promoting Christian Knowledge (ISPCK), Post Box 1585, Kashmere Gate, Delhi-110006.

ISBN: 978-93-90569-58-8

Cover Design: Rev. Dn. Jerin Johnson

Laser typeset by

ISPCK, Post Box 1585, 1654, Madarsa Road, Kashmere Gate, Delhi-110006 • *Tel:* 23866323

e-mail: ashish@ispck.org.in • ella@ispck.org.in
website: www.ispck.org.in

Prayer for the World

"Oh, Prabhu Parameshwar,
Ever compassionate God ....

You are the Paramatman, the Supreme Spirit,
Who is omnipotent, omnipresent, and omniscient,
And in whom we live, move, and have our being.

You are the Sat-Chit-Ananda,
Ever dwelling in the depths of our hearts
As the eternal source of love, peace and joy.

You are the Sadguru who is the Light of the world,
Who leads us from falsehood to truth, from
Darkness to light and from death to immortality.

To you we offer our worship and adoration,
Oh Lord and God, and pray:

Bless all humankind with your grace and peace.

May the world be a joint-family of love
Built on the eternal values
That are common to all religions of humankind.

May the humankind be a global community
Of prayer, fellowship, simplicity and hard work,
Ever seeking for greater fruitfulness.

May courage of conviction, strength of character,
Spirit of adventure and quest for excellence
Be the abiding qualities of this global community.

We make this prayer in the name of Sadguru Jesus Christ
With abiding faith and sure hope
In your eternal love, Oh Prabhu Parameshwar,
Our Lord and our God"

Acharyasri

This book is surrendered to Prabhu Parameshwar, the true God of Light-Love-Spirit, in, with and through my Lord and Divine Master Sadguru Jesus Christ with great joy and gratitude in my heart. It is also dedicated with joy and gratitude to my four gurus.

1. Justice Joseph Vithayathil,

2. Rev. Fr. Bede Griffiths, OSB Cam,

3. Swami Ranganathananda and

4. Mahatma Gandhi

who came into my life at four different stages in my pilgrimage of faith and enabled me to discover the mission of my 'second life' and give practical expression to that mission in the multi-religious and multi-cultural context of India, my beloved motherland.

Acharyasri

Contents

Prayer for the World ... v

Dedication ... vii

A New Creation in Christ ... xiii

The Turning Point ... xvii

Foreword ... xix

Preface ... xxiii

Prologue ... xxix

Introduction ... 1

Joy and Gratitude ... 5

Part One
Foundational Thoughts

Introduction ... 21

1. The Crises Facing India and the World ... 23

2. Lessons Taught by the Pandemic ... 34

3. Mission of India and the Indian Church ... 41

4. Need for an Indian Face of the Christian Faith ... 52

5. Creative Fidelity ... 57

6. Collective Eco-Spiritual Responsibility ... 61

Part Two
An Indian Face of the Christian Faith

Introduction ... 69

Constituent – 1 The Unbound Christ ... 72

Constituent – 2 Open Christianity ... 75

Constituent – 3 The Interreligious Theology ... 82

Constituent – 4 Advaitic Christology ... 93

Constituent – 5 Inclusive Missiology ... 98

Constituent – 6 Liberative Spirituality ... 103

Constituent – 7 Holistic Philosophy ... 119

Constituent – 8 Eco-Spiritual Ideology ... 132

Constituent – 9 Enlightened Christian Leadership ... 143

Constituent – 10 Christian Mission Methodologies ... 149

Constituent – 11 The Peace of Christ Meditation ... 155

Constituent – 12 Fruitful Christian Life ... 159

'Dharma Bharathi Darsana Samhita' ... 162

The Tree of *Dharma Bharathi* ... 165

Part Three
Integral Renaissance of India

Introduction ... 169

1. Navasrushti International ... 172

2. The Integral Renaissance of India ... 178

3. Christusishya Shanti Sangham ... 180

4. Dharma Bharathi Institutes ... 183

5. Dharma Bharathi Mission ... 186

6. Dharma Rajya Vedi ... 188

7. Tyagarchana Shanti Mission ... 191

Appendix A
In Search of the Common Aspects in
Christianity and Hinduism ... 210

Appendix B
Viswa Shanti Peetam ... 225

A New Creation in Christ

"Therefore, if anyone is in Christ, he is a new creation; old things have passed away; behold, all things have become new." (2 Cor 5:17). These words were written by St. Paul from his own personal experiences. From being an enemy of Christ and his disciples, Saul of Tarsus became 'Paul the Apostle', one of the most ardent disciples of Lord Jesus Christ in human history.

St. Paul had further told us that 'God has reconciled us to Himself through our Lord Jesus Christ, and has given us the 'ministry of reconciliation', and that 'God was in Christ reconciling the world to Himself' (2 Cor 5:18-20). Hence, when we are in Christ, we also share with him the ministry of reconciliation.

This latest book 'An Indian Face of the Christian Faith' authored by Acharyasri Dr. Sachidananda Bharathi can be seen as a 'manual' for the mission of reconciliation at all three levels: personal, social and ecological.

At personal level Acharyari speaks about 'forgiveness and reconciliation' as an essential prerequisite to experience and enjoy true peace, joy and abundant life that our Lord Jesus Christ offers to humanity. Acharyasri also developed a 'Peace of Christ Meditation' for this purpose. At social and ecological levels, he has been promoting the 'Tyagarchana Shanti Mission' which is an eco-spiritual mission and interreligious movement for a culture of love, peace and sustainable development in the pandemic-devastated world. Kerala, the cradle of Christianity in the Indian subcontinent, is being presented and promoted by him as the seedbed and pilot project of Tyagarchana Shanti Mission. I am also a part of this eco-spiritual mission and interreligious movement.

The most inspiring aspect of the Tyagarchana Shanti Mission is that though it is centered on the 'cross of Christ', it does not promote any religious conversion. Acharyasri very rightly points out that it is not simply the religion of Christianity that saves humanity from sin and sinful ways but the 'cross of Christ'. Here too, he very clearly points out that a spiritual renewal and moral regeneration of the various Christian Churches are historic imperatives that can be realized only by returning to the 'cross of Christ'. He further states that this much-needed spiritual renewal and moral regeneration of the Christian Churches will be possible only with the power and wisdom of God given to us in, with and through the living Spirit of Christ, the crucified and risen Lord.

I believe that the Holy Spirit today is calling Christians all over the world, more so in India, to a very challenging mission of rebuilding the pandemic-devastated and violence-ridden world on the strong foundation of the grace and truth of God, as well as of the power and wisdom of God, given to us in, with and through our Divine Master, the crucified and risen Christ.

I feel deep within me that all of us will be able to become 'new creations in Christ' and transform India and the world into 'new creations in Christ' only if we are able to put into practice in our own lives the twelve Constituent elements of the 'Indian face of the Christian faith' presented by Acharyasri in this book.

I thank Acharyasri for his prophetic mission in writing this book. I also pray for abundant divine blessings upon all peace-loving people of goodwill who read this book and are inspired to make it a mission manual for becoming 'new creations in Christ'.

Justice (Retd) Kurian Joseph
Former Judge
Supreme Court of India

The Turning Point

By the title 'The Turning Point' I do not mean the bestselling book under the same title written in 1982 by Fritjof Capra. What I wish to present here is the 'turning point' in the life of Acharyasri Dr. Sachidananda Bharathi, the author of this book in your hands.

I have known Acharyasri for more than 3 decades now. My late elder brother, Sri. K P Joseph, was very closely associated with Acharyasri from the very beginning of his mission in 1982, soon after his encounter with death in an air accident. It was the 'turning point' in the life of Acharyasri who was then 'Squadron Leader N V John'. Life has not been the same for him ever since then. It was that 'turning point' which has finally motivated him to take on a spiritual quest which now finds its fruition in, with and through this new book.

His spiritual quest has motivated Acharyasri to write many books. This new book which is in your hands now is the latest among them. This book in itself is a marvel as the readers will see for themselves as they go through it. But, what I wish to share with the readers is the transformation that was brought about in the life of Acharyasri by the 'turning point' in his life.

'Prince John' (as he was known during the early years of his career in the Indian Air Force) was a dynamic, young, ambitious and fun-loving IAF officer. Married in October 1979 to Ms. Lalitha Elizabeth Devasia, an equally dynamic young IRS officer of 1974 batch. They were blessed with a girl child, Deepti Michelle John, in August 1980. The young IAF officer dreamt of starting his own private Air Line & Hovercraft Services in Kerala. It was at such a point of time that he met with an air accident. He was the Navigator of the IAF DC-3 aircraft that had crash landed in the large Dharmapuri lake in Salem District in Tamil Nadu, on 8th July 1982.

Encountering death at the prime of his life, that too at the least expected moment, made Squadron Leader John think deeply about life and its purpose. In his spiritual quest he was blessed with four 'gurus' at four different stages in life. In his semi-autobiographical book 'A New Creation in Christ' written during the initial months of the COVID-19 pandemic Acharyasri has shared about his experiences and experiments in detail.

This new book presents the outlines of the 12 Constituents of the 'Indian face of the Christian faith' developed by Acharyasri over the last four decades. These Constituents, if applied effectively, can become a 'turning point' not only in the history of Christianity but also of humanity.

May this book receive positive and creative responses that it deserves from its readers. May it also become a 'turning point' in the lives of the readers as it contains the fruits of Acharyasri's profound spiritual experiences that had become a 'turning point' in his own life.

K P Fabian, IFS (Retd)
Professor, Symbiosis University, Pune;
Former Ambassador of India to Italy
& National President, Dharma Rajya Vedi

Foreword

In his book titled, "An Indian Face of the Christian Faith", Acharyasri Dr. Sachidananda Bharathi rediscovers the real spirit of Christianity. He redefines Christian discipleship, mission and ministry with reference to the Indian religious pluralistic context. In this book, Acharyasri shares his spiritual insights on harmonious synchronization of Christian spirituality with the religious values of Hinduism. Acharyasri combines his faith experiences in setting his vision and mission.

'What good is it to me if the Son of God was born to Mary unless He is born in me, in my time, in my culture and in my country?' was a radical question that Acharyasri was forced to ask himself. In his quest to find a satisfactory answer to the above mentioned question, four gurus were brought into Acharyasri's life: Justice Joseph Vithayathil, Rev. Fr. Bede Griffiths OSB Cam, Swami Ranganathanandaji, and Mahatma Gandhi. These luminaries influenced Acharyasri at four different stages of his life. He also had opportunities to gain lived-life experiences of the truth, goodness and beauty of four theistic religious traditions such as Christianity, Hinduism, Islam and Sikhism. He was also strongly inspired and influenced by the German mystic Meister Eckhart (1260-1328).

The 'Indian face of the Christian faith' answers life transforming questions that Acharyasri faced in his life journey. This book is also an effort to give practical expression to the 'Indian face of the

Christian faith' for rebuilding the COVID- 19 pandemic-devastated world on a sustainable development paradigm. This is a historic divine mission to promote a culture of love, peace and sustainable development in the pandemic-devastated world, beginning with and from Kerala, the cradle of Christianity in India.

In his search after divine wisdom Acharyasri finds in Jesus Christ the true Divine Master. Acharyasri accepts Jesus Christ as the fullness of divine love, compassion and truth. The divine call of disciples of Jesus Christ in this world is to become more and more Christ-like in their own lives (Rom 8: 29). They are also called to strive prayerfully and incessantly to transform the world into the 'kingdom of God' (*Dharma Rajya*) in answer to the Lord's prayer (Matt 6: 10).

According to Acharyasri, the vision of *Dharma Rajya* can be realized only through an interreligious mission in the multi-religious context of the world. Hence, the vision and mission of *Dharma Rajya* will also need an interreligious philosophy and theology as well as a comprehensive interreligious action plan. The 'Indian face of the Christian faith' is meant to serve as an operational 'mission manual' for the divine task ahead.

Acharyasri developed a creative application of the 'Christu Marga' in the context of the present COVID- 19 pandemic-devastated world as an interreligious sadhana and eco-spiritual ideology of liberation termed 'Tyagarchana'.

The term 'Tyagarchana' comprises two words, 'tyaga' and 'archana'. 'Tyaga' means conscious and willing sacrifice. It is the voluntary renunciation of something that is dear to one's heart. 'Archana' means an offering made to God with love upon the altar of one's own life. Selfless service rendered to our needy fellow human beings with love is the best form of 'Archana' that we can offer to

God. We can see God only in and through others. Hence, serving others with love is serving God with love. *'Manava Seva, Madhava Seva'* (Service to humanity is service to God) is an ancient Indian dictum that reflects this teaching of Jesus Christ. *Tyagarchana* is an inter-religious sadhana and ideology of sacrificial love and selfless service. The eternal ideals that have ever inspired the Indian mind are being put into practical action through *Tyagarchana.*

In this book, Acharyasri emphasizes that "a spiritualization of Christianity by returning to the 'Cross of Christ' is the urgent need of the post pandemic era". Acharyasri believes that such a spiritualization of the Christian faith will constitute the evolutionary growth of Christianity. This must begin with the individual disciples of Jesus Christ who are prepared to share the redemptive mission of the Divine Master through the path of his cross.

The 'cross of Christ' is really the path of forgiving, enduring, and self-sacrificing love. According to Acharyasri, this path of the cross of Jesus Christ is "Sahana Yoga". Mahatma Gandhi understood the divine law of Jesus Christ well and applied it very effectively as 'Satyagraha' for the political freedom of India. He demonstrated to the world the power and wisdom of God in the Cross of Jesus Christ.

I am happy and proud to forward this commendable book of Acharyasri to the public for reflection and appraisal. May the Lord bless Acharyasri and his new vision so that he and his vision become a source of light for many during this era of anguish, darkness and uncertainty.

Dr. Joshua Mar Ignathios
Bishop of Mavelikara;
Vice President I, CBCI,
& President, DRV – Kerala.

Preface

Incarnation of Jesus Christ is a magnificent phenomenon of 'God becoming human' leading to an amazing inculturation of heaven on earth. Eventually, the perspectives towards Gospels that contain the episodic narratives of the life and messages of Jesus became meaningful to different nations and its people, in the context of regional folks and periodic socio-cultural beliefs and practices. Certainly, that enabled the human life to imbibe and to integrate the essence of the Gospel values and to live them according to one's own traditions to attain complacency and fulfillment.

Christianity in India records almost 2000 years of its history. Though Christian faith was introduced in the Indian soil by committed missionaries, and to a larger extent has been very traditional for a long time, subsequently, Christianity in India had witnessed growth in indigenous revival by adopting local cultural elements and faith practices. Current portrayal of Christianity in India as a *'Colonial Foreign Religion'* with alien expressions in its theology, spirituality, faith and traditions needs scholarly reflections and critical thinking.

Authoring of the present book titled, "An Indian Face of the Christian Faith" by Acharyasri Dr. Sachidananda Bharathi outstands as a colossal task in the rediscovery of the real spirit of Christianity, Christian discipleship and towards redefining the mode of Christian mission and ministry with reference to Indian religious pluralistic context.

Through the pages of this book, Acharyasri attempts to share his personal views and spiritual insights and experiences on harmonious synchronization of the in-depth Christian faith and spirituality with the philosophy and culture of Hindu religion and thereby lays emphasis on finding true meaning and fulfillment in one's life. It is evident that Acharyasri combines his deep faith and rich life experiences in setting his vision and mission as well as in activating and achieving them with diligence.

Being an ardent disciple of Lord Jesus Christ, Acharyasri's genuine commitment to "Sadguru Jesus" on one hand and at the same time being a grateful Indian, his earnest longing to project his Indian face of Christianity on the other hand have been clearly reflected in this book. Acharyasri dwells on the mission of clarification and internalization of the values of the Kingdom of God. His implicit faith in the person, life, mission, death and resurrection of Jesus Christ is stunning.

The benevolence of the author is unique as he extends an open invitation to the present and the future generations to become "new creations in Christ", to be equipped with a strong universal focus to transform the pandemic-devastated world into a New Creation in Christ based on an Indian face of the Christian faith with neither religious conversion nor cultural alienation. Conversely, the reader gets that strong flavor of the unquestionable integrity and nobility of Acharyasri all over again as one absolutely gets to feel that he is strongly determined to build a bridge between Christianity and Hinduism avoiding all kinds of inclusive, exclusive and syncretic claims of religions, keeping in mind the cardinal principles of "Forgiveness and Reconciliation".

Acharyasri's vision of 'Indian Face of Christian Faith' is heavily backed up by his understanding of "New Creation in Christ". He has also developed a *'Prabhu Parameshwar'* Theology, a *'Sadguru'* Christology, a *'Dharma Rajya'* Missiology, a *'Sahana Yoga'* Spirituality, a *'Dharmodaya'* philosophy, and a *'Tyagarchana'* eco-spiritual ideology for realizing the vision and fulfilling the mission entrusted to him by his Divine Master.

There is a clear and loud message proclaimed by the book that can be perceived through the following lines wherein Acharyasri says, *"After my reconciliation with the Church in 1984 with the help of my Christian guru Rev. Fr. Bede Griffiths, OSB Cam, there came a stage of learning the rich spiritual and cultural traditions and insights of Christianity and of India and making them my own. This was part of my efforts to rediscover my roots as a disciple of Lord Jesus Christ, my Divine Master, in the multi-religious and multi-cultural context of India, my beloved Motherland. The Divine Master and Mother India became the 'two loves' of my heart. My ongoing spiritual quest thereafter has been to integrate these two loves of my heart into one life-mission that can promote an 'Indian face of the Christian faith' in the multi-religious and multi-cultural context of my country without religious conversion and cultural alienation."* He has been successful in promoting and communicating the multiple facets of the vision and mission to which he is deeply committed. They become inscribed in golden letters in the minds of the reader through his diversified, thought provoking, analytical and captivating lines in this book.

In his 'Joy & Gratitude' Acharyasri takes the reader on a mesmerizing journey through a personal testimony. He explicitly demonstrates his real encounter with Christ and his commitment thereafter to the new vision and mission, and the new life that he accepted and followed.

I had the privilege of releasing his earlier book 'A New Creation in Christ' at Dharma Bharathi Ashram on 08 July 2020. I was also invited to inaugurate a 'New Creation Movement' on that day to usher in the Kingdom of God of love, righteousness, peace and reconciliation on earth. The vision and mission presented in and through that book and that movement are now being given concrete practical expressions in the multi-religious context of the pandemic-devastated world in this new book. I am very glad to write a Preface to this new book.

The contents of this book substantiate how Acharyasri has been relentlessly toiling to achieve his mission through concrete action plans. As the reader goes through the pages, he/she discovers an awesome display of the true virtues that Acharyasri is endowed with namely, love for humanity and sanctity for individuality.

The six chapters in Part-One of this book lay a very strong intellectual foundation for the 12 Constituents of the 'Indian face of the Christian faith' presented in Part-Two of this book.

Acharyasri also presents in Part-Three of this book an Integral Renaissance Movement to transform the pandemic-devastated world into a 'New Creation in Christ' based on the 'Indian face of the Christian faith'. He is convinced that this great mission has to begin with and from India, that too from Kerala, the cradle of Christianity in the Indian subcontinent. He is also deeply convinced that India, especially Kerala, has a leading role to play in rebuilding the pandemic-devastated world on a peace and sustainable development paradigm inspired by a unitive eco-spiritual consciousness.

Acharyasri in this book also points out that just as the institutionalization of Christianity began from the West with Rome as its center, the spiritualization of Christianity must begin from the East with India as its center. Within India itself, it is Kerala that has to be the seedbed and role model of the Indian face of the Christian faith in the pandemic-devastated world. He envisions a 'death and resurrection' of the various morally degenerated Christian Churches in India and the world in order to bring forth a new vision of a spiritualised and divinised Christianity. He also feels that such a new vision of Christianity must find its first practical expression in Kerala. According to him, the COVID-19 pandemic marks a 'turning point' in the history of Christianity in the world, especially in Kerala.

The core and center of Christian faith is a living and loving relationship with the person of Jesus Christ, the crucified and risen Lord. "I am the vine, you are the branches. He who abides in me and I in him, bears much fruit; for without me you can do nothing" (John 15: 5). Acharyasri has made this revelation the core and center of his interreligious mission to promote the 'Indian face of the Christian faith' presented in this book.

The book will be a driving force for the humanity to move forward with a collective responsibility and motivation to overcome the challenges of this era and to live a harmonious and complimentary religious life amidst the religious pluralistic status of the pandemic-devastated world.

The new mission strategy developed and presented by Acharyasri in this book will help the Indian Christianity for a paradigm shift to a creative and unprejudiced Christian mission without losing the true spirit of Christianity.

I wish and pray for showers of divine blessings upon Acharyasri. May this book be an inspiration and guiding light for the present as well as for the future generations.

Dr. Kuriakose Mor Theophilose Metropolitan
President, Ecumenical Commission & Metropolitan, European Bhadrasanam, Malankara Jacobite Syrian Orthodox Church; Resident Metropolitan & Professor, MSOTS; & Chairman, National Council of Mentors, DRV.

Prologue

"An Indian Face of the Christian Faith "is a gift of the Holy Spirit to the pandemic-devastated world through its author Acharyasri Dr Sachidananda Bharathi. Enlightened Indian Christian leaders like Hon. Supreme Court Justice Kurian Joseph, Ambassador K.P. Fabian, Bishop Joshua Mar Ignathios, Dr. Kuriakose Mar Theophilose Metropolitan and Lt. Gen. Ashok Vasudeva, PVSM, AVSM, VSM (Retd) have expressed their great appreciation for the book, its content and the author. The author has shared his experience of a deep and abiding personal communion with the Risen Lord. His first personal encounter was in an Air Force Hospital in October 1982, following an air accident in July the same year. This encounter totally changed this young and dynamic serving Officer of the Indian Air Force. He was never again the same, his priorities became different, his vision of the meaning of life was different, his perception of his calling in the world was different. His experience of communion with the Lord only deepened. This shows the importance and value of the contents of the book.

Part -One, of the book contains six chapters that present the 'Foundational Thoughts' that have gone into the formulation of the 'Indian Face of the Christian Faith' presented in Part-Two.

The twelve Constituents of the Indian Face of the Christian Faith are presented in brief in Part-Two of the book. Together these twelve Constituents also form a new 'School of Thought termed '*Dharma Bharathi Darsana Samhita*' which can provide a strong eco-spiritual foundation for an Integral Renaissance of India presented in Part-Three.

The world today is going through a very critical stage. The COVID-19 Pandemic and the Russia-Ukraine war have added fuel to the fire of human anguish in this era. Our Hindu brothers and sisters speak of 'Avatars' from age to age to liberate humankind from forces of evil and to establish righteousness on earth. The disciples of Lord Jesus Christ deeply affirm that Our Lord carried our sins and died on the cross so that we might die to sin and live for righteousness (1 Pet 1:24). The disciples of Christ are called to protect and promote righteousness in the world, more so at times of crises such as the one that we are going through today.

The author from his forty years of experience as a disciple of Christ in our multi-religious and multi- cultural context of India has been able to develop and present an authentically Christian yet authentically Indian Theology, Christology, Missiology, Spirituality, Philosophy, Ideology and Way of life that can lead to an Integral Renaissance of our beloved country and an Integrated World Order.

The Acharyasri prophesies that the COVID-19 Pandemic marks the end of the old era of 'institutionalization' of Christianity and the beginning of a new era of 'spiritualization' of Christianity. That should make us think of ways and means of making our discipleship of Christ more spiritually meaningful and fruitful in the years ahead for the glory of God and good of humanity.

I express my deep appreciation and extend my prayerful blessings to the author and the book. I thank him and congratulate him for this work.

I hope and pray that the Universal Church, and specially the Indian Church, will be greatly enriched by the contents of this book.

✠Oswald Cardinal Gracias
Archbishop of Bombay & President,
Catholic Bishops' Conference of India
May 31, 2022

Introduction

"Beloved, let us love one another, because love is from God; everyone who loves is born of God and knows God." (1 John 4:7)

Introducing the dance always begins with introducing the dancer. Similarly, introducing the book has to begin with introducing the author. This is not a difficult task for me as Acharyasri and I have been 'soul mates' in the living Spirit of Christ, the Holy Spirit of God, since several years.

My first personal meeting with Acharyasri was five years ago when he was invited by us as a Resource Person in the Annual Conference of our Military Christian Fellowship of which I have been the National President. What impressed me most about him was his rootedness in Christ and his openness to other religions. While many Christian missionaries and pastors have negative attitudes towards other religions and their scriptures, Acharyasri looks at other religions and their scriptures with respect and devotion. At the same time, he is also deeply rooted in his faith in Christ and in the one true God revealed to humankind by Lord Jesus Christ. 'The more one is rooted in the truth, goodness and beauty of one's own religion, the more one will be open to the truth, goodness and beauty present in other religions.' This is what he teaches and preaches. I believe that the world today, especially India, urgently needs such an open approach.

This book aptly titled 'An Indian Face of the Christian Faith' is a remarkable book. It presents the Christian faith in such a way that anyone can accept and live it without religious conversion and cultural alienation. The concepts of 'Unbound Christ' and 'Open Christianity' presented as Constituents 1 & 2 of the 'Indian face of the Christian faith' can be an eye opener for many of us.

The Interreligious Theology, the Advaitic Christology, the Inclusive Missiology, the Liberative Spirituality, the Holistic Philosophy and the Eco-Spiritual Ideology together can provide a strong foundation for a new vision of Christianity in the third millennium.

The 'Enlightened Christian Leadership', the 'Christian Mission Methodologies', the 'Peace of Christ Meditation' and 'Fruitful Christian life' are like the four pillars of an Indian Church that can lead to an Integral Renaissance of India.

The twelve 'Constituents' of the 'Indian face of the Christian faith' presented in Part-Two of this book together constitute a 'Dharma Bharathi' school of thought termed *'Dharma Bharathi Darsana Samhita'* that can usher in the much-needed Integrated World Order of love, peace and sustainable development in the pandemic-devastated world in the fullness of time with divine grace. Part-Three presents an Integral Renaissance Movement for rebuilding the pandemic-devastated world on an eco-spiritual sustainable development paradigm.

All things considered together, this book presents the building blocks of a New Creation in Christ without religious conversion and cultural alienation.

I find this book authentically Indian, authentically Christian and authentically Universal. For disciples of Lord Jesus Christ like many of us living in the multi-religious context of India and who have served long years in the Defense Services of our nation, this book is a 'dream come true'. It will generate and release a tremendous amount of synergy (collective spiritual energy) for the much-needed moral and spiritual regeneration of India.

May God bless Acharyasri who has put in many years of sincere hard work for developing the twelve Constituents of the 'Indian face of the Christian faith' presented in Part-Two of this book.

May God also bless all readers of this book and make them effective divine instruments for transforming the pandemic-devastated world into the Kingdom of God of righteousness, peace and joy in the Holy Spirit inspired by the 'Indian face of the Christian faith' presented in this book. May God bless all of us.

Lt. Gen. Ashok Vasudeva, PVSM, AVSM, VSM (Retd)
National President, Military Christian Fellowship,
& National Vice President, Dharma Rajya Vedi

Joy and Gratitude

"Rejoice always, pray continually and give thanks in all circumstances; for this is God's will for you in Christ Jesus." (1 Thessalonians 5: 16-18).

"Eternal life is knowing the one true God and Jesus Christ whom He has sent." (John 17:3).

This book is surrendered to *Prabhu Parameshwar*, the one true God of Light-Love-Spirit, in, with and through my Lord and Divine Master Sadguru Jesus Christ with great joy and gratitude in my heart. It is also dedicated to my four gurus; Justice Joseph Vithayathil, Rev. Fr. Bede Griffiths, OSB Cam, Swami Ranganathananda, and Mahatma Gandhi who came into my life at four different stages in my pilgrimage of faith and enabled me to discover the mission of my 'second life' and give practical expression to that mission in the multi-religious and multi-cultural context of India, my beloved motherland.

This book is the fruit of 40 years of my pilgrimage of faith as a disciple of Sadguru Jesus Christ in the Indian soil following the divine guidance, I received through my four gurus.

08 July 2022 is the 40th anniversary of my encounter with death in an air accident that had changed my life radically. I was

a 35-year old ambitious and fun-loving officer of the Indian Air Force at the time of that air accident. I was hospitalized following the air accident. It was in the Air Force Hospital at Bengaluru that I had my first personal encounter with the living Spirit of Christ. Life has not been the same for me ever since.

I have written the story of my 'pilgrimage of faith' covering a period of 38 years (from 1982 to 2020) in detail in my book 'A New Creation in Christ' which was authored during the first year of my confinement to Dharma Bharathi Ashram due to the COVID-19 pandemic. The book was released and dedicated to God at Dharma Bharathi Ashram on 08 July 2020, the 38th anniversary of my air accident.

This new book in your hands is a prayerful attempt to express my joy and gratitude for the great and wonderful ways in which the living Spirit of Christ has been guiding me in my 'second life'. I have been inspired to transform my spiritual insights and experiences into an 'Indian face of the Christian faith' for rebuilding the pandemic-devastated world on the strong foundation of an eco-spiritual peace and sustainable development paradigm with the power and wisdom of God given to me in, with and through the living Spirit of Christ. To help the readers, understand this mission and the inspirations behind it better I am sharing below some of the important milestones in my pilgrimage of faith as a disciple of Sadguru Jesus Christ in the multi-religious and multi-cultural context of India, wherein Divine Providence has given me birth.

An important step that I was inspired to take after my first personal encounter with the living Spirit of Christ in 1982 was to seek reconciliation with the Church. Though I was born and brought up in a traditional Syro Malabar Christian family, I was alienated from the Church since my early youthful years. I had wrongly identified Lord Jesus Christ with the Church at that time.

As a result, I had also attributed the failures and weaknesses of the Church to Lord Jesus Christ as his own failures and weaknesses. But when I came to realize that the Church is only a community of weak and sinful men and women like me trying to follow the Divine Master and find their refuge and strength in the Holy Spirit offered to his disciples by him, I could empathize with the Church and be part of it willingly and consciously.

After my reconciliation with the Church in 1984 with the help of my Christian guru Rev. Fr. Bede Griffiths, OSB Cam, there came a stage of learning the rich spiritual and cultural traditions and insights of Christianity and of India and making them my own. This was part of my efforts to rediscover my roots as a disciple of Lord Jesus Christ, my Divine Master, in the multi-religious and multi-cultural context of India, my beloved Motherland. The Divine Master and Mother India became the 'two loves' of my heart. My ongoing spiritual quest thereafter has been to integrate these two loves of my heart into one life-mission that can promote an 'Indian face of the Christian faith' in the multi-religious and multi-cultural context of my country without religious conversion and cultural alienation.

With the publication of this book, which is in your hands now, my ongoing spiritual quest has entered its final phase. My one and only mission hereafter will be to promote among interested people what is written in this book and to prepare a cadre of visionary-missionaries to rebuild the pandemic-devastated and violence-ridden world on the strong foundation of the 12 Constituents of the 'Indian face of the Christian faith' presented in Part-Two of this book as *Dharma Bharathi Darsana Samhita*.

Kerala, the cradle of Christianity in the Indian subcontinent, is taken as a seedbed and pilot project in this historic divine mission of the third millennium.

The most important discovery made by me as a disciple of Sadguru Jesus Christ is the discovery of my own identity as an 'eternal spiritual being' (as a 'god') with a unique eco-spiritual mission in this world. This realization has been inspiring me to use the grace and truth as well as power and wisdom of God given to me in, with and through Lord Jesus Christ, my Divine Master, for the glory of God and good of humanity, beginning with and from India, the country of my birth. 'What good is it to me if the Son of God was born to Mary unless he is born in me, in my time, in my culture and in my country?' was a question that I was forced to ask myself, drawing inspiration from the German mystic Meister Eckhart (1260-1328). It has taken forty years (1982-2022) for me to find ways and means of responding creatively to this life-transforming question. Part-Two of this book sums up and presents the 12 Constituents of the 'Indian face of the Christian faith' developed by me over the decades based on the results of my spiritual quests and experimental initiatives. The 'Indian face of the Christian faith' constitutes a new 'school of thought' which is termed *'Dharma Bharathi Darsana Samhita'*. The twelve Constituents of the 'Indian face of the Christian faith' also constitute the twelve elements of *'Dharma Bharathi Darsana Samhita'*. Part-Three of this book presents six practical expressions of the *'Dharma Bharathi Darsana Samhita'*.

Four gurus were brought into my life by Divine Providence (Justice Joseph Vithayathil, Rev. Fr. Bede Griffiths OSB Cam, Swami Ranganathananda & Mahatma Gandhi) at four different stages in my pilgrimage of faith to find a satisfactory answer to the life-transforming question mentioned above. I also had opportunities to gain lived-life experiences of the truth, goodness and beauty of the four theistic religious traditions in India (Christianity, Hinduism, Islam & Sikhism).

My answer to the above-mentioned question constitutes the 'Indian face of the Christian faith' (also termed *Dharma Bharathi Darsana Samhita*) presented in this book. This book is also an effort to give practical expression to the 'Indian face of the Christian faith' for rebuilding the pandemic-devastated world on an eco-spiritual peace and sustainable development paradigm. This is a historic divine mission of the third millennium, beginning with and from India with focus on Kerala, the cradle of the Christian faith in the Indian subcontinent.

*   *   *   *   *   *   *   *

In my personal life as a disciple of the Divine Master in the multi-religious and multi-cultural context of India I have also been undergoing changes from time to time. My original name at the beginning of my mission was Squadron Leader N V John. I was initiated into spiritual life with the new name 'John Sachidanand' on 08 July 1984, the second anniversary of my air accident. I received a 'Baptism of Spirit' back into the Catholic Church on 25 November 1984, my 37th birthday, under this new name. I left the Indian Air Force on 31 May 1989 with the permission of my wife Smt. Lalitha John, IRS, and spent three months in silence and prayer with my guru, Rev. Fr. Bede Griffiths, OSB Cam, in his Saccidananda Ashram near Tiruchirappally in Tamil Nadu. I wrote my first book *'Pratyasa Dharma Samhita'* during that period of silence and prayer. It had contained the vision and mission of my 'second life' in a seminal form. This *'Dharma Bharathi Darsana Samhita'* which is in your hands now contains the vision and mission of my 'second life' in their fully developed form.

I was given 'Acharya diksha' by my guru on 18 January 1990 in Saccidananda Ashram. This marked the beginning of the mission of my 'second life'. I was called to be an ardent disciple of Lord

Jesus Christ in the multi-religious and multi-cultural context of India. I was also called to be a visionary-teacher and a dedicated missionary of an 'Indian face of the Christian faith' without religious conversion and cultural alienation, following the footsteps of my Divine Master, Sadguru Jesus Christ who was a Jew and remained a Jew till his death on the cross.

I was inspired to leave home and family, and to give up private property in 1996 with the written permission of my wife who was at that time serving as an Additional Commissioner of Central Excise & Customs (She was an IRS officer from the 1974 Batch) at Coimbatore.

After 5 years of life as a *parivrajaka* (homeless mendicant) I entered a life of *Sanyasa* on 25 July 2001, the 50th birthday of my wife. Here also, I had taken her permission.

On 25 November 2001, my 54th birthday, I had received two sets of saffron dress (one old and one new) from my 3rd guru Swami Ranganathananda at Belur Math, the Headquarters of Ramakrishna Mission near Kolkata. Swamiji was the International President of Ramakrishna Mission at that time. I also had shaved off my head following his example. All these things happened in a very miraculous way about which I have written in chapter-4 (Experimental initiative No.14) of my earlier book 'A New Creation in Christ'.

I initiated the *'Bharathi' Chaturashrama Sanyasa Parampara* on 08 July 2003, the 21st anniversary of my air accident, and took the name 'Swami Sachidananda Bharathi'. Thereafter I felt being totally guided by the living Spirit of Christ. The *Sanyasa* stage of my life came to an end on 02 October 2020.

With effect from 02 October 2020, the 151st birthday of Mahatma Gandhi, my 4th guru, I have entered the last and final stage of my pilgrimage of faith on earth dressed in pure white with the simple name 'Acharyasri'. This is envisaged to be the '*Ativarna Ashrama*' stage of life after the *Sanyasa* stage. This final stage is meant to be a stage of final summing up and integration of one's life and mission on earth. 'White' is the colour of truth, purity and integration.

Thus, I have gone through all stages of human life according to India's rich and inspiring socio-cultural traditions. To be rooted deep in the socio-cultural traditions of 'my land and my people' has also been an integral part of the divine mission entrusted to me by my Divine Master.

Lord Jesus Christ was ever working all through his life. "My Father is always working, and I too must work" (Jn 5: 17), he had told his disciples. We, the disciples of this Divine Master, must also be ever dynamic and creative. In this process, one will also find that everything is being integrated into ever newer, higher and larger missions till it is brought to its final 'perfection' in Christ. I see this Christian perfection as the final goal and destiny of every disciple of Christ.

By giving up something dear to oneself for the sake of a higher goal, one is gaining much more than what was given up. Nothing good that has ever been thought, said or done with love for the glory of God and good of humanity will ever go wasted or be lost. It will be entered in the 'Book of life' and will be deposited in the 'Bank of eternity'. It will also be integrated into greater goals and higher mission in future.

The vision and mission realized in his being and preached on earth by Lord Jesus Christ was the 'Kingdom of God'. The term 'Kingdom of God' (or 'Kingdom of Heaven') appears more than 100 times in the New Testament. The Divine Master also told his disciples: "Seek first the kingdom of God and His righteousness, everything else shall also be given to you." (Matt 6: 33).

The 'Kingdom of God' preached by Lord Jesus Christ is being referred to by us as '*Dharma Rajya*' from an Indian socio-religious perspective. Kingdom of God is not something to be achieved after death through good works done on earth in this life. It must begin within and among us, here and now in this world. It is a life of righteousness, peace and joy in the Holy Spirit (Rom 14: 17).

'He carried our sins on his body and died on the cross, so that we might die to sin and live for righteousness' (1 Peter 2; 24) was the insight of St. Peter, the 'rock' upon which the Divine Master had laid the foundation of his 'Church'. This is a call and mission for every disciple of the Divine Master to be an 'avatar', a protector and promoter of righteousness on earth, with the power and wisdom of God in Christ.

The divine call of every disciple of Lord Jesus Christ in this world is to become more and more Christ-like in his/her own life (Rom8: 29). We are also called to strive prayerfully, tirelessly, fearlessly and incessantly to transform the world into the 'Kingdom of God' (*Dharma Rajya*) in answer to the Lord's prayer (Matt 6: 10).

The vision of *Dharma Rajya* can be realized only through an interreligious mission in the multi-religious context of the world. Hence, the vision and mission of *Dharma Rajya* will also need an interreligious Theology, Christology, Missiology, Spirituality, Philosophy and Ideology as well as a comprehensive interreligious action plan. These are now developed well and are presented briefly in Part-Two of this book as the 12 Constituents of the 'Indian face of the Christian faith' ('*Dharma Bharathi Darsana Samhita*').

A well-formulated vision and mission constitutes a goal to be achieved. A goal broken down into steps becomes a plan. A plan needs to be backed up with concrete action programmes. This is an ongoing process. Hence, I have written several books and have been involved in many projects and movements over the years. These are summed up and presented in my previous book 'A New Creation in Christ' published in 2020.

All that is required now is to build the super structure upon the strong foundation already laid by the living Spirit of Christ in, with and through me during the last forty years. This book in your hands is meant to serve as a 'mission manual' for the divine mission ahead. What is written by me in this book on any subject supersedes what was written on the same subject by me earlier in any other book, if there is any discrepancy between the two.

It has been my experience over the years that if we are to be guided by the Holy Spirit, we have to be ever ready to give up many old habits, traditions, ideas, systems and institutions, as well as dogmas, doctrines and 'sacraments'. We also have to be ever ready to accept new ones from time to time. This will also mean that we cannot afford to be attached permanently to habits, traditions, ideas, systems, organizations or institutions, dogmas, doctrines and sacraments of the past, however dear and attractive they might be, if we must be truthful to our call for a dynamic and creative eco-spiritual life and mission. We need to be constantly moving forward, upward and Godward. Creative fidelity, not repetitive loyalty, is what is required of a disciple of Lord Jesus Christ who is being guided by the Holy Spirit. Such a disciple of Christ has to be ever dynamic and ever creative.

The National Ecumenical Symposium on *Mission of Christian Churches in Post-Pandemic India* organized on 27 November 2020 at Dharma Bharathi Ashram inspired a new content and orientation for my vision and mission. I have come to the firm conviction that a spiritualization of Christianity by returning to the 'Cross of

Christ' is the crying need for rebuilding the pandemic-devastated and violence-ridden world.

I also believe that a spiritualization of Christianity based on the Cross of Christ will constitute the next stage in the evolutionary growth of Christianity as a global religion. This has to begin with the individual disciples of the Divine Master who are prepared to share the redemptive mission of their Lord through the path of 'cross' which is the path of forgiving, enduring, and self-sacrificing love. I have termed this Christian path of forgiving, enduring and self-sacrificing love as *'Sahana Yoga'*.

The institutionalization of Christianity from the West with Rome as its center was the first stage in the redemptive mission of Sadguru Jesus Christ. With the COVID-19 pandemic that first stage has come to an end and a new stage in the evolutionary growth of the Christian faith has begun. This will be a stage of spiritualization of Christianity in which India has to play an important role. Within India itself, it will be Kerala, the cradle of Christianity in the Indian soil, that will have to take the lead and show the way as a 'second Israel'. The first Israel had given birth to Jesus Christ, the Saviour of humankind. The second Israel has to serve as a divine instrument to rebuild the pandemic-devastated and violence-ridden world on the strong foundation of that Saviour's living Spirit.

*   *   *   *   *   *   *   *

This book is given the subtitle *'Dharma Bharathi Darsana Samhita'* because the 'Indian face of the Christian faith' presented in this book is also termed 'Dharma Bharathi' school of thought for human solidarity, holistic development and integral peace. *'Dharma Bharathi Darshana Samhita'* means 'Dharma Bharathi' school of thought.

The term *'Dharma Bharathi'* implies the Power (Force) or the Divine Master driving the chariot of 'Light of Righteousness' on earth as explained in chapter-1 of Part-three of this book. The Power (Force) is Mother India and the Divine Master is Sadguru Jesus Christ. The *'Dharma Bharathi Darsana Samhita'* is the fruit of an integration of these 'two loves' of my heart.

This book contains three parts and two appendixes. Part-One consists of six chapters presenting the 'foundational thoughts' leading to the 'Indian face of the Christian faith'.

Part-Two consists of the 12 Constituents of the 'Indian face of the Christian faith' which is also termed *'Dharma Bharathi Darsana Samhita'*.

Part-Three presents an Integral Renaissance of India based on the 'Indian face of the Christian faith' / *'Dharma Bharathi Darsana Samhita'*. This is a practical application of the 'Indian face of the Christian faith' to rebuild the pandemic-devastated India on an eco-spiritual peace and sustainable development paradigm.

Appendix-A to this book includes an Article written by Rev. Dr. Adai Jacob Cor Episcopa. This Article will help the readers to understand the common meeting points of Christianity and Hinduism at a deeper level. It will also enable us to be more effective instruments of God in promoting the 'Indian face of the Christian faith' through Hindu-Christian dialogue and cooperation. Appendix-B presents the vision of a World Peace Center termed 'Viswa Shanti Peetam'.

I am deeply grateful to H E Oswald Cardinal Gracias for his inspiring message. The Cardinal has been a great promoter of interreligious dialogue. His words of encouragement and appreciation will surely add to the effectiveness of the vision and mission presented by me in and through this book.

Hon. Justice Kurian Joseph, a former Judge of the Supreme Court of India with great integrity of character and courage of conviction, has pointed out in his Prologue to this book titled 'A New Creation in Christ': *"I feel deep within me that all of us will be able to become 'new creations in Christ' and transform India and the world into 'new creations in Christ' only if we are able to put into practice in our own lives the twelve Constituent elements of the 'Indian face of the Christian faith' presented by Acharyasri in this book."* Coming from him, these words mean a lot to us. I thank and praise God for the gift that Hon. Justice Kurian Joseph has been to me and to India and the Catholic Church.

My esteemed 'friend, philosopher and guide' Ambassador K P Fabian has sent a very inspiring Message to be included in this book under the heading 'The Turning Point'. I thank Ambassador Fabian for the love and whole-hearted support that he has been extending to me and the mission in which we are now co-workers and fellow pilgrims.

I thank Most Rev. Joshua Mar Ignathios for his inspiring Foreword and Dr. Kuriakose Mor Theophilose Metropolitan for his inspiring Preface to this book. Both are men of God dear to my heart. They occupy important positions in their respective Churches. May they and their Churches be blessed abundantly by the power and wisdom of God in Christ Jesus our Divine Master.

One of the highly decorated Army Generals, Lt. Gen. Ashok Vasuveda, PVSM, AVSM, VSM (Rtd) has written an Introduction to this book. He has been a source of inspiration and strength for me. I am ever grateful to him. I pray for abundant divine blessings upon him and his family, and upon the Indian Army.

I express my heartfelt gratitude to Rev. Dr. Adai Jacob Cor Episcopa for his spiritual companionship and for his wholehearted support to our divine mission. His Article, *'In Search of Common Aspects in Christianity and Hinduism'* included as Appendix-A to this book will be very useful for all of us who are inspired to take up the mission of promoting the 'Indian face of the Christian faith' in the multi-religious context of India wherein the majority of people are followers of Hinduism.

I am ever grateful to Acharya Catherine Prabhujyothi, DCP, the Mataji of Dharma Bharathi Ashram, for her spiritual companionship and editorial work. She has been editing most of my books and articles very painstakingly. Her mastery of English language and her study and exposure to pastoral work both in India and America have been of great help to me.

The mission entrusted to us at this juncture in human history is indeed very challenging. But we know that the best things in life are got only at the cost of great pain. The life of selfless service, the suffering death on the cross, and the resurrection from the dead of our Divine Master will always remain sources of inspiration and strength for us in our own life and mission. The Holy Spirit given to us by God in, with and through our Lord Jesus Christ will enable us to fulfill our divinely ordained mission, however challenging and difficult it may be.

Acharyasri
'Guru Bhavan'
Dharma Bharathi Ashram
Perumpilly, Mulanthuruthy, Kochi-682314

PART ONE
FOUNDATIONAL THOUGHTS

Introduction ... 21

1. The Crises Facing India and the World ... 23

2. Lessons Taught by the Pandemic ... 34

3. Mission of India and the Indian Church ... 41

4. Need for an Indian Face of the Christian Faith ... 52

5. Creative Fidelity ... 57

6. Collective Eco-Spiritual Responsibility ... 61

Introduction

Part–One of our book presents the Foundational Thoughts that have gone into the final formulation of the 'Indian face of the Christian faith' presented in Part-Two. The 6 chapters constituting Part-One together provide a strong intellectual and scientific foundation for the 'Indian face of the Christian faith'.

Chapter-1 of Part-One presents the five major crises facing India and the world today seen from a socio-spiritual perspective.

Chapter-2 presents the important lessons taught by the COVID-19 pandemic. Chapter-3 presents the Mission of India & the Indian Church in rebuilding the pandemic-devastated world.

Chapter-4 presents the various 'faces' acquired by the Christian faith over the last two millennia of its evolutionary growth. It also stresses the need for an 'Indian face' for the Christian faith.

The importance of 'creative fidelity' is emphasized in chapter-5. It is also pointed out in this chapter that 'repetitive loyalty' kills all creativity and blocks spiritual growth and development.

Chapter-6, the last chapter in Part-One, presents the concept of 'Collective Eco-Spiritual Responsibility'(CESR) which calls all peace-loving people of goodwill on earth to join hands in fulfilling their collective eco-spiritual responsibility of rebuilding the pandemic-devastated and violence-ridden world on a peace and sustainable development paradigm. The need to develop a Unitive Eco-Spiritual Consciousness is also emphasized in the last chapter of Part-One.

1

The Crises Facing India and the World

'The Limits to Growth' is a 1972 Report of the study by computer stimulation conducted on the exponential economic and population growth with finite supply of resources. This study was commissioned by the 'Club of Rome', an international think tank consisting of global thought leaders sharing a common concern for the future of humanity and planet Earth.

Despite the findings of this study, the 'advanced' nations of the world with their GDP-based developmental concepts, market-driven economic policies and power-oriented political agendas continued, and are continuing, in a direction totally opposed to the findings of the study commissioned by the Club of Rome.

The growing culture of consumerism and materialism denies the unity of all life and the need to abide by ethical and moral values for the common good of all members of the Earth family. It also rejects the solidarity of humankind, and the existence of an omnipotent, omniscient and omnipresent Ultimate Truth, God, who is the source of all creation and ground of all existence, and 'in whom we live, move and have our being'. It places the egoistic little 'self' as the goal and center of all human endeavors and development initiatives.

Both consumerism and materialism are inherently selfish and violent. They have seeds of destructive competition and violent conflicts embedded within them. History bears witness to the truth that ideologies like Communism, Capitalism and Socialism at their core are proponents of consumerism and materialism and hence, they cannot help us find lasting peace and true happiness in life or sustainable development on earth.

The pleasure-seeking and profit-motivated consumerism and the self-centered and spirit-negating materialism today are destroying the dignity of human life and the ecological well-being of Mother Earth. Consumerism and materialism have become the biggest enemies of sustainable human development and lasting global peace. They are also enemies of abiding peace and true happiness within and among individuals, families, communities and nations all over the world today.

Consumerism promotes a 'use and throw' culture. It flourishes in a 'market economy' which can thrive only on an ever-increasing competition and unlimited consumption. It has developed a 'profit, pleasure and power for me at any cost' attitude among its protagonists. Consumerism also promotes corruption and cut-throat competition to capture the market, to make more profits, to enjoy more pleasures and to eliminate the competitors in one's quest for power. 'Development' is measured in terms of consumption today. The more a society or a nation is able to consume, the more developed it is considered to be.

Thus, an increasing slavery to the pleasure-seeking consumerism and self-centered materialism with its ensuing corruption, competition, conflicts and total disregard for ethical and moral values, constitutes the most serious crisis facing humanity today.

*   *   *   *   *   *   *   *

It is a sad reality that more than 60% of the scientists, engineers and technicians in the world today are full-time engaged in development, production and maintenance of weapons of mutual destruction. Major portions of national budgets of many countries all over the world, including that of India, are set apart for this purpose.

The United States of America is supposed to be the most 'advanced' and the most 'powerful' nation in the world today. The American economy is sustained mostly by the 'arms industry'. If its weapons are not sold, America cannot sustain its present level of wasteful consumption and its powerful control over the nations of the world. Consumption and control go hand in hand. They can be sustained only through violence.

There is an ongoing and ever increasing competition among the nation states and multi-national companies for gaining control over the resources of the world.

The 'advanced nations' of the world that together constitute less than 15% of the world's population are consuming more than half of the world's resources today. This is also true for India. 10% of India's population consisting of the rich and the powerful are controlling and consuming almost half of the nation's resources.

Many multinational companies in the present world own wealth more than the wealth of a number of nations put together. Many individuals and families in India today own wealth more than the total wealth of millions of their fellow countrymen put together.

The disparity between the rich millionaires and poor millions all over the world is ever widening and is fast reaching a 'point of no return'. (This is more evident in the present pandemic-devastated world.) The ecological harmony and wellbeing of Mother Earth are being destroyed by the insatiable greed of man. Pandemics and natural calamities have their roots in indiscriminate destruction of ecological harmony and in human greed and pride. There is no justice in the economic systems and no sustainability in the models of development that are being adopted and promoted by many nations including India in the present pandemic-devastated world.

The unjust concentration of wealth and power in the hands of the rich and the privileged few, and the increasing disparity between the rich and the poor constitute the second major crisis facing India and the world today.

*   *   *   *   *   *   *   *

Peace (*Shanti*) in the world needs justice (*neeti*) and righteousness (*dharma*). Justice is based on laws which in turn are based on Constitutions of nation states. It differentiates the human beings from the animals. Righteousness is based on faith and moral values. It elevates the human to the divine.

Justice without righteousness and righteousness without justice cannot lead us to peace and sustainable development. The Government of a nation will have to work to promote economic, social, ecological and political justice in the country. Religions will have to work together to promote ethical, moral and spiritual values based on faith and righteousness.

Justice and righteousness are like the 'two wings' of peace. Justice is the realm of politics and righteousness is the realm of religion. They have to work together if a nation is to find sustainable development and abiding peace and happiness. It was this truth that prompted Mahatma Gandhi to point out that 'those who say religion has nothing to do with politics do not know what religion or politics really is'.

Economics and politics are the two systems that affect almost all dimensions and aspects of human life in the world today. They are interdependent and interrelated. All economic decisions today are political decisions. All political decisions are based on economic considerations. Politics and economics today are controlled by the rich and powerful minority. As a result, the vast majority of people all over the world today are suffering from dehumanizing poverty and malnutrition, and from lack of adequate healthcare and education. Both economics and politics need to be humanized and spiritualized. They must also be made value-based. This is an urgent and very important task ahead of religions today.

Spiritual and moral values promoted by religions are very essential to humanize and spiritualize economics and politics for the common good. Unfortunately, a growing moral degeneration and a wide-spread spiritual apathy have afflicted all religions of humanity today. Hence, they have become incapable of playing their destined role in the divine plan. There is also a demand today for keeping religion and politics separate. At the same time, there exists an unholy alliance between them for gaining power and privileges for their own selfish advantage.

The moral degeneration of religion and politics, and the diabolical alliance between degenerated religion and degenerated politics constitute yet another major crisis facing India and the world today.

*   *   *   *   *   *   *   *

Peace is a prerequisite for sustainable development. There is hardly any peace in the world today. A living and loving relationship with the one true God, the source of our being and ground of all existence, is a prerequisite for true and abiding peace. *'Know God, know peace. No God, no peace'* is an ancient dictum with great wisdom.

The God we worship determines our character, value system, worldview and relationships. Our understanding of God has to lead to an ever growing and ever deepening experience of the oneness of reality. One's understanding of God also has to undergo an on-going deepening and broadening process with growth in wisdom and expansion in consciousness.

Most religions are still clinging on to totally outdated concepts and images of God, often opposed to reason and discoveries of science. As a result, these religions fail to inspire their followers to adhere to abiding ethical and moral values without which peace and happiness in the world are impossible. Such religions also become more and more intolerant of other religions. Religious fanaticism and violence will also increase when religions stop growing spiritually as co-pilgrims in the path of truth and peace.

God is the Ultimate Reality, the Source of all life and Ground of all existence. This Ultimate Reality is the Supreme Spirit from whom all creation comes forth, and in whom all creation exists and finds its fulfillment. Human beings are spiritual beings with physical bodies, created in the image and likeness of God who is the source of all Wisdom (Light), Mercy (Love) and Power (Spirit).

Every human person has within himself/herself immense resources of divinity. Religions are meant to help their followers to understand and channelize these divine resources to make their lives more fruitful, peaceful, dynamic and happy in this world. Unfortunately, the understanding of life and reality and the concepts and images of God presented and promoted by most religions in the world are irrelevant to the contextual realities of human existence today. It is said by the wise that not having any conception of God is better than having a wrong conception.

There is an urgent need for religions in the world, more so for religions in India, to undergo a 'death and resurrection' process today and be spiritually reborn with an integral vision of life and reality. Only then can they be relevant to the realities of human existence in the present era. Such spiritually regenerated religions alone can play their destined role effectively in the life and destiny of India and the world.

Many people today are clinging on to the wrong and irrelevant images of self and God and to a disintegrated vision of life and reality promoted by age-old and outdated religious traditions and belief systems. As a result, there is a growing moral and spiritual decay all over the world today. This in turn leads to increasing corruption, injustice, insecurity, intolerance, communalism, fanaticism and terrorism. Religions are afflicted by a growing 'moral cancer'. For India, this moral and spiritual crisis facing religions can have dangerous consequences as vast majority of the people in this country are ignorantly, yet deeply religious. Popular religiosity influences people in India today more than true spirituality.

The wrong and irrelevant images of self and God and a disintegrated vision of life and reality promoted by age-old and outdated religious traditions and belief systems is yet another serious crisis facing India and the world today.

*   *   *   *   *   *   *   *

The root cause of almost all problems facing humanity today is the disintegration of human consciousness caused by a four-fold alienation of man: alienation from his own inner self, alienation from God, alienation from his fellow human beings and alienation from Nature. Hence, a 'unitive eco-spiritual consciousness' gained through a four-fold reconciliation: reconciliation with self, reconciliation with God, reconciliation with fellow human beings and reconciliation with Nature, is an essential prerequisite for the much-needed moral and spiritual regeneration of India and the world. It is also a prerequisite for sustainable development and abiding peace on earth.

God is the all-pervasive Supreme Spirit who is omnipotent, omnipresent and omniscient. Unitive eco-spiritual consciousness is the consciousness of the spiritual unity underlying all apparent physical diversities in the world. It enables one to see 'God in All and All in God'. It inspires us to see the whole humankind as one large family bound with a common destiny. It enables us to see the interdependent organic nature of planet Earth. It prompts us to accept the different nation states and religious communities in the world as smaller families within the larger human family. Such a unitive eco-spiritual consciousness is the only way to human solidarity and sustainable development, and to true peace and happiness for the human race in this world.

Reconciliation with one's own inner self is the first step in the four-fold reconciliation necessary for developing a unitive eco-spiritual consciousness and hence, for experiencing true peace and happiness. If there is no peace within individuals, there will not be peace among people in the world. Peace within the individual is the 'seed' of peace in the world. This calls for repentance, forgiveness and reconciliation. We need to repent for our 'sins' of commissions and omissions and seek forgiveness from others for the offences we have committed against them. We also need to forgive others their offences committed against us.

Repentance, forgiveness and reconciliation will enable us to experience inner peace. This in turn will help us grow and advance in our quest for a unitive eco-spiritual consciousness. We will then be able to discover our true spiritual nature and divine potentials. Our religious faith and practices should help us to find and experience this inner peace through repentance, forgiveness and reconciliation.

God is the omnipresent, omnipotent and omniscient Supreme Spirit in whom we live, move and have our being. He is the source of all life and ground of all existence. God has no gender, though we traditionally use masculine terms to refer to God.

God can be experienced as an ocean of infinite love, mercy and compassion. Reconciliation with God implies understanding the true nature of God and our existence in Him, and experiencing His love, mercy and compassion. This will enable us to become more loving, merciful and compassionate persons. This is the second step in the four-fold reconciliation needed today. Our religious faith and practices should help us to experience this reconciliation with God, and thus to become more loving, merciful and compassionate human beings.

It is in the human person that life becomes conscious and mind enters into the realm of spirit, and spirit itself displays its divine nature and potentials. The Spirit of God dwells within every human person. Hence all human beings are to be treated with respect and love. We need to become conscious of the God who dwells within the heart of every human person. We also need to see ourselves in and through others. We have to forgive others and seek forgiveness from others and live in harmony and peace with others. This is the basis of reconciliation with fellow human beings. Helping their followers to come to such an understanding is also an important task of religions. Building a culture of peace in the world is the common mission ahead of religions in the world.

Creation is God's Self-expression bound with space and time. The Spirit of God pervades and permeates the whole creation.

Hence, creation and all life in it are sacred. Earth is a common 'mother' to all living beings inhabiting this planet. Mother Earth is a living organism the health and vitality of which will depend on the health and vitality of her individual parts. Polluting her air, water or soil is doing harm to ourselves. Humankind and all other living beings together constitute an 'Earth Family'. This 'Earth Family Consciousness' is the basis of reconciliation with nature.

An alienation of people from their own inner selves, from God, from one another and from Nature is yet another serious crisis facing India and the world today. Added to this malady is the absence of the much-needed Earth Family Consciousness.

*   *   *   *   *   *   *   *

The five serious crises facing India and the world today, as they are outlined above in this chapter, can be summed up as follows:

1. Increasing slavery to consumerism and materialism and total disregard for ethical and moral values.

2. Unjust concentration of wealth and power in the hands of the rich and the privileged few and the increasing disparity between the rich and the poor.

3. Spiritual degeneration of religions and politics, and a diabolical alliance between the degenerated religions and degenerated politics.

4. Wrong images of self and God, and a disintegrated vision of life and reality.

5. Alienation of people from their own inner selves, from God, from one another and from Nature.

The crises facing India and the world as they are mentioned above are not exhaustive, they are only indicative. We have only tried to comprehend the major crises facing the nation and the world in this present era from an eco-spiritual perspective.

*   *   *   *   *   *   *   *

The ever-loving and eternally forgiving and merciful God places a seed of opportunity in every crisis facing us individually or/and collectively. The natural calamities and pandemics facing India and the world have within them the seeds of a New Creation based on an integral vision of life and reality. Our religious faith and practices will have to be deepened and broadened so that they can help us to discover these seeds, and make them sprout, grow and bear abundant fruits in the world. Helping their followers to develop a unitive eco-spiritual consciousness that sees 'God in all and all in God' is the challenging task of the era ahead of all religions. Only those religions that can rise to meet this challenge alone deserve to survive. Others will have to die their natural death sooner or later.

2

Lessons Taught by the Pandemic

To fulfill our divinely ordained mission in the pandemic-devastated world, we will have to heed to the lessons taught by the COVID-19 pandemic. What are the important lessons taught by the pandemic? The vision to be adopted and the mission to be undertaken by us in this era in order to overcome the crises facing India and the world as seen in the previous chapter will very much depend on the correct answer to this question.

First of all, the COVID-19 pandemic has shown to us the limits of human knowledge and power. The mighty nations of the world with their large stockpiles of deadly bombs and missiles and with their powerful leaders have proved to be miserably helpless in front of the microscopic COVID-19 virus! The whole world today is still reeling under the fear and agony unleashed by the pandemic. The sufferings, deaths, and destructions caused by the COVID-19 pandemic have been beyond the imagination of most people.

Humankind shall surely survive this tragedy. We shall overcome this crisis sooner or later with the grace, wisdom, power and mercy of God. However, humanity will emerge from this crucible of suffering much more humbled and purified than ever before. We will also have to seek forgiveness for our many past sins of commissions and omissions against our fellow human beings, against other species of living beings in the Earth-Family and against Mother Earth, our 'common mother' who nurtures and nourishes all living beings. Above all, we need to amend our ways of thinking and living. Our attitudes and relationships also need to undergo radical changes.

The solidarity of humankind, the unity of all life and the interdependent organic nature of planet Earth are three of the very important lessons taught by the COVID-19 pandemic. We have come to realize the truth that humanity is a large family bound with a common destiny. We, the humans, are also part of a large 'web of life' and planet Earth is a common 'mother' to all living beings. As the most advanced species among the many species of living beings sharing this planetary home, we humans need to take care of the air, water, and soil of Mother Earth and learn to live in harmony with all other species of living beings sharing this 'Common Home'.

Scientific studies have proved that the strain on the resources of Mother Earth to support one non-vegetarian individual is much more than that of supporting an individual with vegetarian food habits. Studies have also shown that human beings are basically meant to be vegetarians in their food habits. The need to live at peace and in harmony with Nature and all other living beings sharing our planetary home is a lesson that the COVID-19 pandemic has taught us in the hard way.

Human beings are body-soul-spirit entities. Just as the body has many organs like the eyes, nose, mouth, ears, lungs, heart, stomach, hands, legs etc., the soul also has many faculties like thinking, discerning, intellect, imagination, will, memory, feelings, emotions etc. Similarly, the spirit also has various gifts, fruits and attributes. A human person is the total sum of all these and more.

This holistic and integral understanding of the human person is being lost to us today. We are now living in an era of 'specializations'. We look at the physical, mental and spiritual dimensions of life as distinct and separate from one another. We also see that the secular and the sacred, the feminine and the masculine, the rational and the intuitive, as if they are opposed to each other. A rediscovery of an integral vision of life and reality is the crying need of the pandemic-devastated world of the present era. We also need to develop an 'Earth Family Consciousness'.

We have to understand that economic prosperity, political power and military strength cannot help us find true peace, happiness and sustainable development. Neither physical development nor material wealth alone can help us discover the true meaning and purpose of human life in this world. They can only be the means, but not the end. Just as breathing and eating are essential for life but are not the goals of life, physical development and material wealth are essential for life, but cannot be the goals of life.

The consumerist culture and materialistic philosophy also cannot lead us to the true meaning and purpose of human life. The transcendent spiritual dimension is much more important than the immanent physical, mental and material dimensions. This is yet another important lesson taught by the COVID-19 pandemic.

The religious, political, economic, social and ecological dimensions of human life in this world are interrelated and interdependent. Such a holistic vision of life and reality is also lost to us today. The pandemic-devastated world needs an urgent rediscovery of a holistic vision of life.

We have also come to realize the truth that most religions and their scriptures, codes, creeds, cults and sacraments, as they are being interpreted, understood and practiced today, will have very little relevance to the realities of human life in future. All sectarian interests, divisions, conflicts, competitions, and violence based on religions, religious books or religious issues and rituals are fruits of the dehumanizing forces of selfishness, insecurity, fear, greed, ignorance and superstitions working in the lives of the followers of different religions. The COVID-19 pandemic has made it an important and urgent imperative for us to liberate ourselves from such an ignorant religiosity based on these dehumanizing elements. Openness to the truth, goodness and beauty within oneself and in other individuals, cultures and religions is an attribute of a truly spiritual person. Developing such an open 'secular' spirituality is an important task ahead of us today.

The COVID-19 pandemic has also taught us the limitations of science and technology. Many atheists, just like religious fanatics, have been claiming that science and technology could solve all human problems, and hence, they should replace God and religion. This claim has also proved to be only an expression of human ignorance, ego and 'scientific' superstition.

Science and technology have surely helped to make the physical existence of humankind more comfortable, fast and productive. They have also helped the advanced nations and rich people to exploit the resources of the world in greater measures for their own advantage. Science and technology have further helped the nations of the world to develop deadly weapons of mutual destruction. But they could not stop the deaths and devastations caused by a tiny virus like the COVID-19! Even the richest and most advanced nation in the world today, the United States of America, with its great wealth and unmatched scientific developments has proved to be totally helpless in front of the tiny COVID-19 virus. It simply means that science and technology do not and cannot have answers for all problems facing humanity. They also cannot replace God and religion. Hence, while accepting and using them as efficient means for improving the quality of physical life of humankind, we also need to be fully aware of their limitations. We need to be very humble when dealing with the mysteries of human life and of the universe, and of the divine forces operating within and behind them.

We have come to realize that the various ideologies in the present world like Capitalism, Communism and Socialism are outdated ideologies based on an outdated worldview. None of these ideologies is based on the solidarity of humankind, the unity of all life and the interdependent organic nature of planet Earth; the three most important lessons taught by the pandemic. Hence, they can never help us discover the true meaning and purpose of human life or establish a culture of peace and sustainable development on earth. The pandemic-devastated world urgently needs an eco-spiritual ideology rooted in and inspired by the solidarity of humankind, the unity of all life and the interdependent organic nature of planet Earth. It also has to be an ideology that can spiritualize economics and politics, and rebuild science and technology on the new foundation of love.

We have also come to realize that the Ultimate Reality, the one true God, is beyond all institutionalized religions, written scriptures and scientific discoveries. These can, at their best, be only pointers to the one true God in whom we live, move and have our being. This one true God will forever remain above and beyond all names, forms, and attributes imagined or can ever be imagined by human mind.

Human beings constitute one of the many species of living beings inhabiting the planet Earth which is just one of the planets in our Solar System. Our Solar System itself is only one among the millions of Solar Systems in our Galaxy, the Milky Way. The Milky

Way is also just one among the millions and millions of Galaxies in the Universe. The size of the Universe will always remain far beyond the reach of the little man's brain and its comprehending capacity. This means that we need to develop an ever greater amount of humility in these matters. Science and technology can find their true direction and meaning only if they are based on such an ever increasing degree of humility and ever greater sense of mystery.

We will need the grace, power, wisdom and mercy of God to rebuild our broken lives and ruined world on a new holistic eco-spiritual peace and sustainable development paradigm.

The real crises facing India and the world today presented in chapter-1 above are authenticated to a large extent by the lessons taught by the COVID-19 pandemic.

We are called today to transcend all divisive and sectarian worldviews, attitudes, and ideologies to enter into a new era of an enlightened unitive eco-spiritual consciousness with an integral vision of life and reality. This is our destined divine call and mission in this era.

Of all the nations in the world, it is to India that the world turns for help at this crucial period in human history. India is called to take the lead in the mission of presenting a peace and sustainable development paradigm based on a unitive eco-spiritual consciousness to the pandemic-devastated world.

Of all the religions in the world, it is Christianity that is called to lead the religions in the world in the mission of ushering in the Kingdom of God of love, righteousness, peace and reconciliation on earth.

The following two chapters (chapters -3 & 4) will help us understand the historic calls and missions of India and the Indian

Church in the pandemic-devastated world. These two individual calls and missions of India and the Indian Church are being integrated into one global mission in, with and through the 'Indian face of the Christian faith' presented in Part-Two of this book.

3

Mission of India
and the Indian Church

Just as individuals and communities have their specific tasks to perform in the divine plan, nations and religions also have their destined roles to play in the evolutionary growth of human consciousness. In this chapter our efforts are focused on discovering the roles destined for India and the Indian Church in the divine plan.

A.   Call and the Mission of India

Of all the nations in the world, it is India that can present a 'counter culture' to the loveless, violent consumerism and spirit-negating selfish materialism that are eating into the soul of humanity today. However, India is not able to play her destined role in the divine plan as she herself is enslaved by a number of negative and self-destructive forces.

As we have already seen, the real crises facing India and the world today are not economic and political alone, but have deeper moral and spiritual dimensions that are much more serious than the economic and political crises. Hence, an Integral Renaissance of the human race that can bring about a much-needed spiritual and moral regeneration of the religious, economic, political, ecological and social dimensions of human life in the pandemic-devastated world is the crying need of the era. This has to begin from and with the pandemic-devastated India. An 'Integral Renaissance' that can bring about the much-needed spiritual and moral regeneration of the religious, economic, political, ecological and social dimensions of India's national life is the crying need of the era (*Yuga Dharma*) for India to survive as a dynamic living force in order to fulfill her destined mission in the divine plan.

India alone has the potential to present a 'counter culture' to the loveless and violent consumerism and spirit-negating selfish materialism in the pandemic-devastated world. The seeds of such a counter culture are already available to 'We, the People of India' in abundance within our own rich spiritual and cultural traditions. India is also the cradle of an Earth Family Consciousness in the world. A study of the *enlightened* spiritual and cultural traditions of India will prove beyond doubts the authenticity of such a claim.

India has been a land of religions that sought after Truth (*Satya*) and Non-violence (*Ahimsa*) incessantly from the beginning of history. Righteousness (*Dharma*), Renunciation (*Tyaga*), and action without any selfish desire (*Nishkama Karma*) have been her eternal ideals. Peace (*Shanti*) has been always her goal and in all things. All her prayers concluded with *"Shanti.... Shanti.... Shanti..."* to signify the three dimensions of abiding peace encompassing the personal, social and ecological dimensions of human life in this world.

The Indian culture and thought are deeply religious. Religion has been playing a very important role in the lives of most Indians. Art and architecture, music and dance… all have religion as their basis in this ancient land of religions. Nothing in India really grows unless it touches the religious sense of the Indian people.

All religions of the world have their living presence in India. Five world religions were born in her own soil ('*Sanatana Dharma*' or the Eternal Religion, Buddhism, Jainism, Hinduism & Sikhism). Out of these, the *Sanatana Dharma* can be seen as the 'mother' of all other four religions (Buddhism, Jainism, Hinduism & Sikhism) born in India. Other religions like Judaism, Zoroastrianism, Christianity, Islam and Bahai were warmly welcomed and accepted by India into her loving fold. This spiritual hospitality of India had perhaps earned her the name 'Mother India'. A mother is an embodiment of forgiving, enduring and self-sacrificing love. Mother's love is the closest to divine love in the world.

*   *   *   *   *   *   *   *

A story is told that when Hitler invaded Poland during World War-II, 500 Polish women and 200 children were put into a ship by the Polish Army. The Captain was told to take them to any country that accepted them. The ship was not given permission to enter their ports by any of the European countries. After many months of being refused by all countries the ship reached the Port of Iran. There too it was refused entry. Finally wandering over the sea, it reached Bombay. The British Governor refused to allow the ship to enter the Port of Bombay.

The Maharaja of Jamnagar, Jam Saheb Digvijay Singhji Jadeja, heard the news. He welcomed the ship to Jamnagar. He gave free hospitality to the women and children. He also gave free education to the children in his Army School for nine years till they were able to return to Poland after World War II. One of those children later became the Prime Minister of Poland. The descendants of those who were given shelter by Maharaja 'Jam Saheb' still remember with gratitude the warm hospitality of the Indian Raja. They make annual pilgrimages to Jamnagar even today. Many roads in Warsaw are named after Maharaja Jam Saheb whom the Polish people had been calling 'Bapu' with love and gratitude. This is just one example of the hospitality of India from modern history. We have similar inspiring stories about how the Parsis, Jews, Christians and Muslims were accepted into her loving fold by 'Mother India'.

*   *   *   *   *   *   *   *

'Bharat Mata'/ 'Mother India' has been nurturing an ecological worldview and Earth Family Consciousness from the beginning of history. *'Vasudhaiva Kutumbakam'* (Earth is one family), proclaimed the Rishis and Sages of this ancient land of religions. *'Loka samastha sukhino bavanthu'* (May the whole world live in happiness) was their prayer.

'Ekam sat vipra bahudhavadanti' (Truth is one, wise men and saints refer to it by various names) was India's understanding of God and Truth. *'Isavasyamidamsarvam'* (God pervades and lives in the whole creation) was her experience. *'Ahimsa paramo dharma'* (Non-violence is the highest virtue) was her proclamation of faith. *'Satyameva jayate'* (Truth alone will succeed) is the National Motto of India.

India has been a land of saints and sages. The great and holy men and women of India have always been individuals of *tyaga* (renunciation). Renunciation and service have been the eternal ideals ever cherished by India. The *Rishi*, not the *Raja*, had been India's ideal. All things considered, India seems to have been set apart by Divine Providence for the mission of ushering in a culture of truth, righteousness and peace on earth through interreligious dialogue and cooperative action.

"At this supremely dangerous moment in human history, the only way of salvation for mankind is the Indian way. Emperor Ashoka's and Mahatma Gandhi's principle of non-violence, and Sri

Ramakrishna's testimony to the harmony of religions: here we have the attitude and spirit that can make it possible for human race to grow together into a single family, and in this atomic age, this is the only alternative to destroying ourselves." These words of Arnold Toynbee (1889 – 1975), one of the greatest historians of modern era, point to the very important and urgent role that India is called to play in building a great new world of peace and sustainable development on the strong foundation of an eco-spiritual consciousness. India has a very important role to play in promoting the much-needed 'unitive eco-spiritual consciousness' and a 'collective eco-spiritual responsibility' for rebuilding the pandemic-devastated world on an abiding peace and sustainable development paradigm.

B.   Call and the Mission of the Indian Church

There can be no peace in the world without righteousness and there can be no righteousness in the world without the moral and spiritual values. Promoting moral and spiritual values among their followers is the primary responsibility of religions. In the multi-religious context of India and the world, interreligious dialogue and cooperation are very essential to promote righteousness and peace.

Dr. S Radhakrishnan, the late philosopher President of India, whose birth day (5th September) we celebrate every year as 'Teachers' Day', after his deep study of world religions came to the conclusion that religions can come together for a culture of peace in the world only if there is a shared and inclusive vision and mission among them. Well-known theologian Dr. Hans Kung had also pointed out that there can be no peace in the world without peace among religions in the world.

Of all the religions in the world, it is Christianity that can promote a global vision and mission which will help to establish a much-needed civilization of love and culture of peace in the world based on the dignity and divinity of the human person. This global mission of Christianity will have to begin with and from the Indian Church. To fulfill her destined mission in the divine plan, the Indian Church will have to undergo a death and resurrection process in order to give birth to a spiritualized Christianity in place of the Institutionalized 'Churchianity' in India and the world today.

The Indian Church will have to become the 'salt of the earth and light of the world' for the much-needed Integral Renaissance of India. She will have to pay the price for bringing about such an Integral Renaissance of India with her own sweat, tears and blood; sweat of selfless hard work, tears of ardent prayers, and blood that is shed in non-violent struggles for the economic, social and moral freedoms that are yet to be won for India as pointed out by Mahatma Gandhi in a letter written on 27 January 1948, just three days before his martyrdom. This mission calls for a 'marriage' of religion and science, of the religious East and the scientific West, as propounded by my guru Rev. Fr. Bede Griffiths OSB Cam in his epoch-making books titled 'The Marriage of East and West' and 'A New Vision of Reality'.

The marriage of East and West will imply at its deepest level a 'spiritual marriage' between Christianity and Hinduism that will bring forth an 'Indian face of the Christian faith' without religious conversion and cultural alienation based on an integral vision of life and reality and a synthesis of science and spirituality.

I was fortunate to be a disciple of Bede Griffiths and was given the name 'John Sachidanand' in 1984 and *Acharya deeksha* in 1990 by him in order to be a living testimony to this 'spiritual marriage' of Hinduism and Christianity at the deepest level. I was entrusted with the mission of promoting this spiritual marriage of East and West as the mission of my 'second life'. I was 'initiated' by him to bear testimony in my own life and mission to such a Hindu-Christian spiritual marriage.

During the initial months of the pandemic, I was inspired to write a semi-autobiographic book titled 'A New Creation in Christ' in which I have summed up the story of my 38 years of Christian discipleship in a multi-religious and multi-cultural context of India, and my quest for a civilization of love and culture of peace in India and the world. This book was released and dedicated to God in Christ in our Dharma Bharathi Ashram on 08 July 2020, (the 38th anniversary of my air accident and first encounter with the living Spirit of Christ in 1982), by my esteemed friend, Dr. Kuriakose Mor Theophilose Metropolitan of the Malankara Jacobite Syrian Orthodox Church, who has also kindly written the preface to this book. On that day, he had also initiated a global movement termed 'New Creation Movement' inspired by the book 'A New Creation in Christ'.

In the context of the present conflict-ridden world all peace-loving people of goodwill from different religious traditions of humankind need to unite in the mission of promoting a culture of reconciliation and peace on earth. The Indian Church nourished by the rich spiritual and cultural traditions of India will have to take the lead and show the way, in spite of her many weaknesses.

It is by working prayerfully, tirelessly and fearlessly for peace that we become true sons and daughters of God. *"Blessed are the peacemakers, they will be called the children of God"* (Matt 5: 9), taught Lord Jesus Christ, the Prince of Peace. In other words, a peace-building mission enables us to become true sons and daughters of God. This truth makes peace-building the most important mission and vocation for disciples of the Divine Master. Peace-building is the mission mandate for them from their Lord.

"Peace be with you. As the Father has sent me, so do I send you" (John 20: 21). This was the mission entrusted to his disciples by Sadguru Jesus Christ.

We need to remember always that in today's globalized world no country, culture, or religion can ever remain an island by itself or work in isolation. All countries, all cultures, and all religions are unique, but are interrelated, interdependent and interconnected. We are all part of the 'web of life'. We together constitute a 'global network of relationships'. This is also a truth reminded to us in a very painful way by the COVID-19 pandemic. Hence, while our action can be local, our vision needs to be always global. Our vision of God and our understanding of reality also have to be open, inclusive, interreligious and universal.

*　　*　　*　　*　　*　　*　　*　　*

"Gandhi was probably the first person in history to lift the love ethic of Jesus above mere interaction between individuals to a powerful and effective social force on a large scale. The intellectual and moral satisfaction that I failed to gain from the utilitarianism of Bentham and Mill, the revolutionary methods of Marx and Lenin, the social contract theory of Hobbes, the 'back to nature' optimism of Rousseau, and the superman philosophy of Nietzsche, I found in the non-violent resistance philosophy of Gandhi", pointed out Dr. Martin Luther King Jr.

Mahatma Gandhi can provide a direction and model for the modern world, more so for disciples of Sadguru Jesus Christ, to be effective instruments of reconciliation and peace in the multi-religious context of the world. However, the disciples of the Divine Master will have to undergo a spiritual and moral regeneration first and be rooted deep in the rich spiritual and cultural traditions of India as Gandhi himself was, if they have to be effective in this divine mission of the third millennium. This is an essential prerequisite for disciples of Lord Jesus Christ in the pandemic-devastated India.

*　　*　　*　　*　　*　　*　　*　　*

What one can see from all that is mentioned above, is that the era ahead will be an Indian era. However, in order to be effective in her divine mission, India will have to rediscover her own rich and universal spiritual roots and rebuild herself upon them. A peace and sustainable development paradigm based on a scientific 'unitive eco-spiritual consciousness' will be India's greatest contribution to humanity in the present era. It is also an urgent need for her own very survival and growth as a living spiritual force capable of fulfilling the divine mission entrusted to her by history and destiny.

Only through interreligious dialogue and cooperation can India become an effective instrument of God for bringing forth a new hope for the pandemic-devastated humanity. She will have to present an effective 'counter-culture' to consumerism and materialism. Awakening and empowering India to fulfill her destined role in the world family of nations is the call and mission of religions in India, especially of the Indian Church today.

Humanity's evolutionary growth is directed towards an all-inclusive Unitive Eco-Spiritual Consciousness, which is the consciousness of the eco-spiritual unity underlying all apparent diversities in the physical world. It is the source and basis of an Earth Family Consciousness. It will awaken us to our unity with God and with the whole creation. This is the final goal and destiny of every human being. It will also enable us to enter a living and loving communion with God following the example of Lord Jesus Christ, who was one with God, the Father of all humankind (Jn 14: 10). The evolutionary growth of human consciousness is directed towards this final destiny in God's plan which is also a call to become a 'new creation in Christ'. The pandemic-devastated humanity is poised for such a 'millennium leap' forward in the evolutionary growth of its collective consciousness. India, especially the Indian Church, has a very important role to play in this 'millennium leap' forward of humanity's collective consciousness. However, it is a sad reality that both India and the Indian Church today are unable to respond to their divine calls and missions.

India is enslaved by the evil forces of the dehumanizing poverty, widespread unemployment, all-pervasive corruption, degrading caste system, and ever-growing communalism, as well as by the shameful illiteracy and ill health of her poor millions. She urgently needs an Integral Renaissance to liberate herself from these negative and destructive forces enslaving her today. These forces enslaving our country are only the external visible symptoms of the internal cancerous moral decay and spiritual apathy that have afflicted the soul of India. Hence, what the pandemic-devastated India urgently needs is an Integral Renaissance which can bring about a moral and spiritual regeneration of the religious, economic, political, ecological and social dimensions of her national life.

India is not meant to live for herself. She has a universal mission to fulfill. Take away this universal mission from her, and India will wither and die. The sad reality is that India today is in a 'spiritual coma'. An all-pervasive moral and spiritual degeneration has afflicted her soul. She needs to become a 'New Creation in Christ' with the power and wisdom of God, if she is to survive as a living spiritual force and fulfill her global mission.

The next chapter presents the need and urgency of an 'Indian face' for the Christian faith in order to awaken India and the Indian Church to their destined roles.

Part-Two of this book presents the outlines of an 'Indian face of the Christian faith' that can help in liberating both the Indian Church and the Indian Republic from their slavery to the forces of evil that are enslaving them today, and empower them to play their destined roles in the divine plan.

4

Need for an Indian Face of the Christian Faith

'Christian faith' implies a faith in the person, vision, mission and message of Lord Jesus Christ. It depends on one's understanding of the person of Lord Jesus Christ and one's relationship with the living Spirit of Christ. This is an evolutionary process guided by the Holy Spirit who is the Spirit of Truth given to humanity by Divine Providence. The Holy Spirit leads us to an ever deeper understanding of the one true God, and of the person, vision, mission and message of Jesus Christ whom He has sent.

"Eternal life is knowing the one true God and Jesus Christ whom He has sent" (John 17: 3), says the Holy Bible.

'Christian faith' begins with an abiding faith in the one true God revealed to humanity by Lord Jesus Christ in, with and through his own life and being (John 1: 18). It is faith that leads us to an intimate personal relationship with the one true God as an ever loving, eternally forgiving, and infinitely compassionate 'Father in Heaven' as demonstrated and taught to the world by the Divine Master. It is also the faith that accepts and acknowledges Lord Jesus Christ as the 'Word of God' incarnated in human history (John 1:

14). Christian faith further implies accepting and acknowledging Lord Jesus Christ as the 'human face of God' in history (John 14: 9) and as 'the way, the truth and the life' in humanity's eternal quest for God (John 14: 6).

Christian faith has acquired a number of 'faces' in its evolutionary growth over the last two millennia. The first was a 'Jewish face' which had presented Jesus of Nazareth as the 'Lamb of God, who takes away the sins of the world'. This Jewish 'face' was given to Jesus of Nazareth based on the Old Testament narrative of the 'fall and redemption' of humankind and the concepts of 'original sin' and the sacrifices required to satisfy 'divine justice'.

Then came the 'Roman face' which had presented Jesus of Nazareth as the 'king' of the Jews and the 'saviour' of humankind. The Jews were under the Roman rule at that time. They were eagerly waiting for a powerful leader to liberate them from the Roman subjugation. Many of his disciples and followers had expected Jesus of Nazareth to be such a liberator-king. Judas Iscariot who betrayed the Divine Master was one of the foremost among such disciples.

However, it was the 'Greek face' that had enabled the Christian faith to open to the non-Jewish world by presenting Jesus of Nazareth as the *'Christos'* and *'Logos'*. The Greek word *'Christos'* implies the 'anointed one of God'. The English word 'Christ' has its origin in this Greek word. The Greek word *'Logos'* implies the 'Word of God'. In Indian terms it implies *Sabda Brahman* or *Aadi Shabda,* the Primordial Word that is God.

After a few centuries emerged the exclusive 'Colonial face' of Christian faith that proclaimed Christianity as the 'only true religion' and the Bible as the 'only true Word of God' and Jesus of Nazareth as the 'only Son of God'. Such exclusive claims led to conflicts and violence. Saving the souls of 'pagans' by converting them to this colonial version of Christianity became a self-proclaimed obsession for European Christian missionaries and their counterparts and followers all over the world. This exclusive 'Colonial face' which satisfies the religious ego of its proponents is the most widely spread face of the Christian faith in the world today. This is because the European colonial powers had conquered and ruled over a large number of countries in the world. Christian missionaries with the help and support of these colonial powers succeeded in spreading the 'Colonial face' of the Christian faith all over the world.

The latest face of the Christian faith is the 'Commercial face'. It has its roots in a competitive consumerist culture. This 'Commercial face' proclaims Lord Jesus Christ as the Lord of health and wealth, and as the giver of all good things in life. It makes 'preaching the Gospel' a highly commercial and profitable enterprise with a great deal of sound and fury. Kerala, the cradle of consumerism in India, is a very fertile ground for this version of the Christian faith. One only has to visit any of the many Charismatic Retreat Centers and Prayer Houses in Kerala to understand this truth.

The Christian faith that is being promoted in India today by various Christian Churches is based on one or more of the above five 'faces' acquired by it over the centuries of its evolutionary growth.

Unfortunately, none of the above five faces of the Christian faith appeals to the religious-minded educated Indians because these are not in full harmony with neither the teachings of Lord Jesus Christ nor with India's religious genius that has ever been seeking for God, truth and non-violence incessantly with an open mind based on an Earth Family Consciousness.

Dr. E Stanley Jones, one of the great American missionaries, who had understood well both India's spiritual worth and the essential spiritual power of the Gospel of Lord Jesus Christ, had pointed out in his book 'Christ of the Indian Road':

> "The religious genius of India is the richest in the world. The forms that it has taken have often been the most extravagant, sometimes degrading and cruel. Those forms are falling away, or will fall away, but the spirit persists and will be poured through other forms. As that genius pours through Christian moulds, it will enrich the collective expression of Christianity. But in order to do that the Indian must remain Indian. He must stand in the stream of India's culture and life, and let the force of that stream go through his soul so that the expression of his Christianity will essentially be Eastern and not Western. This does not mean that Indian Christianity will be denied what is best in Western thought and life, for when firmly planted on its own soil it can then lift its antennae to the heavens and catch the voices of the world. But it must be particular before it can be universal. Only thus will it be creative – a voice, not an echo."

Like Dr. Stanley Jones, many disciples of Lord Jesus Christ in India, including me, have felt the need and urgency for an 'Indian face' of the Christian faith without religious conversion and cultural alienation.

Indian spirituality and India's religious quest at their best have been emphasizing the need for a culture of interiority in prayer. Lord Jesus Christ also taught his disciples to go into their rooms, close the doors and pray in silence (Matt 6: 6). A culture of simplicity and renunciation in the lifestyles of religious leaders and spiritual masters was practiced and emphasized in India as exemplified by Lord Buddha, Sri Ramakrishna Paramahamsa, Swami Vivekananda, Sree Narayana Guru, Mahatma Gandhi and such other great men and women of this ancient land of religions. The pomp and show of many Christian leaders and the sound and fury of many Christian prayer groups as well as the consumerist culture of many Christian communities are totally alien to the religious genius of India.

India urgently needs an authentic Christian faith and culture in harmony with her own rich cultural and spiritual traditions and insights. Such an 'Indianized' Christian faith and culture must be creatively expressed in terms, symbols and concepts that can be easily understood and assimilated by the religious-minded people of India, especially by the educated and thinking Hindus. It must also be rooted deep in the four Gospels.

5

Creative Fidelity

The crises facing India and the world, the lessons taught by the COVID-19 pandemic, the mission of India and the Indian Church in the pandemic-devastated and violence-devastated world, and the urgent need for an 'Indian face of the Christian faith' as outlined in the previous four chapters call for well-studied, well-planned and bold creative responses, not emotionally-charged reckless reactions.

1. Repetitive Loyalty

Problems are natural outcome of problematic thinking. What we see depends on where we stand. If our thinking is divisive, there will be problems. The solutions for the problems facing us cannot be found at the same level of thinking that had created those problems. This is a fact experienced by all those involved in finding creative solutions to the various problems facing us individually or collectively. This is an important discovery and statement made by Dr. Albert Einstein, one of the greatest scientists of modern era who had also said, "We stand on the shoulders of the giants of the past".

Most of us are comfortable with traditional ways of thinking and acting. We find security in our 'traditions'. We tend to glorify them. Such glorifications of traditions also compensate for some of the failures of those traditions and help to erase some of our 'guilt feelings'.

'Repetitive loyalty' implies a total adherence to the traditions without critically analyzing the real contributions made by them to our individual/collective growth, to abiding peace and true happiness of the human race, and to sustainable development of the Earth Family (*Vasudhaivakutumbakam*). It also implies repeating verbatim the written or spoken words without applying our intellect, imagination and creativity towards making them relevant to our own time-space milieu. This is the secure 'path of least resistance' that most of us prefer to follow. But this path of 'repetitive loyalty' does not contribute towards finding any lasting solutions to the problems facing us. However, most people prefer to follow this beaten track of 'repetitive loyalty'.

People of 'repetitive loyalty' will repeat the words and ideas received by them from other sources without taking into account the existing context and need. This will lead to lethargy, monotony and boredom. Such an approach kills individual initiative and creativity. The pandemic-devastated and violence-ridden world as well as India and the Indian Church today call for imagination and creativity of very high order, not mere 'repetitive loyalty'.

## 2.	Creative Fidelity

Keeping the eternal truths/basic principles always at the back of our minds, we need to reinterpret them in the light of our expanded consciousness and the consequent improved level of our thinking in order to make them relevant to the context of our present life and to the existing socio-cultural realities. We also have to strive continuously to expand our consciousness and raise the level of our thinking. This is the path of true growth and development.

This is also a scientific principle behind all great human initiatives and achievements.

In order to respond effectively to the problems and crises facing us from time to time, and to find right and lasting solutions for those problems, we need to adopt 'creative fidelity' instead of 'repetitive loyalty'.

'Creative fidelity' implies reinterpreting creatively the insights and revelations presented in Scriptures, and taught by various religious leaders and spiritual masters, and the discoveries made by our scientists and social thinkers in the past, according to the present context of our life based on the needs of the time/place/ culture.

People of 'creative fidelity' are expected to be courageous enough to use their own experience, initiative, imagination and creativity to reinterpret the words and ideas they have received from other sources and people, however venerated/venerable they might be, in order to make them relevant to their own lives, times and social realities. The present world urgently needs such men and women of 'creative fidelity'.

I have often used the term 'sovereign spiritual persons' when referring to men and women of 'creative fidelity' of high order because they are partakers in the unfolding and ongoing creative function of God, the omnipresent, omnipotent and omniscient Supreme Spirit which is the Ultimate Reality that is the Source of all Creation and Ground of all Existence. Such 'sovereign spiritual persons' are 'gods' created in the 'image and likeness' of God the Supreme Spirit. Every human person is called to become such a sovereign spiritual person/son or daughter of God, following the example and footsteps of Sadguru Jesus Christ, the Son of God.

A creative reinterpretation of the Person and mission of Lord Jesus Christ in the Pandemic-devastated and violence-ridden world is the crying need of the hour.

While other religions are founded by great Prophets and Saints and/or based on their Scriptures, Christianity is founded on the person of Jesus Christ and is nourished and nurtured by the living Spirit of Christ, the Holy Spirit of God. This makes Christianity quite different from all other religions of the world. The 'Christian Faith' is a faith in the person of Lord Jesus Christ and in the one true God of Light-Love-Spirit revealed by him, in him, with him and through him.

Creative interpretation of the message and mission of Lord Jesus Christ demands a return to his original vision and mission of the 'Kingdom of God' that was realized by him in his own life and being first, and preached by him on earth during the three years of his active ministry.

The term 'Kingdom of God' ('Kingdom of Heaven') appears more than 100 times in the Gospels. It represented the vision and mission of Lord Jesus Christ in this world. It is not something to be realized after death. It is something to be realized by us while alive, to be realized here and today.

The 'Indian face of the Christian faith' presented in Part-Two of this book is a creative reinterpretation of the person, message and mission of Lord Jesus Christ in the context of the pandemic-devastated and violence-ridden present world.

6

Collective Eco-Spiritual Responsibility

The crises facing India and the world, the lessons taught by the COVID-19 pandemic, the call and mission of India and the Indian Church, the need for an 'Indian face of the Christian faith' and the creative fidelity of high order which is the need of the present era outlined in the previous five chapters call for a global eco-spiritual and interreligious movement. It calls for a collective effort by all peace-loving men and women of goodwill on earth for rebuilding the pandemic-devastated world on the strong and sustainable foundation of an integral vision of life and reality and a synthesis of science and spirituality. This is the 'Collective Eco-Spiritual Responsibility' (CESR) ahead of the human race in the present world.

The concept of 'Corporate Socio-Spiritual Responsibility' (CSSR) developed and promoted by us in 2019 was modified in 2020 as 'Collective Socio-Spiritual Responsibility'. It is now further modified as 'Collective Eco-Spiritual Responsibility' (CESR) in the light of further studies and reflections.

The concept of CESR is inspired by the fact that ecology and spirituality will have to be at the core and center of our efforts to rebuild the pandemic-devastated and violence-ridden world. We also have to understand the fact that the modern world needs more of science and spirituality and less of politics and religion.

We desperately need today a peace and sustainable development paradigm based on an integral vision of life and reality, and an eco-spiritual ideology for rebuilding the pandemic-devastated and violence-ridden world. The concept of 'CESR' is developed by us inspired by this need of the present era.

We have already seen that planet Earth is a living organism, the health and vitality of which will depend on the health and vitality of its individual parts. We human beings constitute the most advanced species of living beings inhabiting this planet. Hence, we have a divinely-ordained responsibility and mission to serve as loving and caring elder brothers and sisters to all other species of living beings sharing our 'Common Planetary Home' in the Solar system which is only one of the millions of such solar systems constituting our Galaxy, the Milky Way which in turn is just one of the millions and millions of Galaxies in the Unfolding Universe. The Universe as we perceive it today is only a very minute part of Creation which is the Self-Expression of God bound with time and space.

Discoveries of modern science and the insights of mystics and saints of humanity have proved that there is an abiding spiritual unity underlying all apparent physical diversities in the world. This underlying spiritual unity is the strongest foundation upon which a culture of love, peace and sustainable development can be built in the pandemic-devastated world.

The solidarity of humankind, the unity of all life, the interdependent organic nature of the planet Earth, and the oneness of the Ultimate Reality constitute the 'four pillars' of an 'Integrated

World Order' which is a historic imperative for a culture of love, peace and sustainable development to emerge for humankind.

The concept of 'Collective Eco-Spiritual Responsibility' implies the collective responsibility entrusted to all peace-loving people of goodwill on earth today by history and destiny to join hands in rebuilding the pandemic-devastated and violence-ridden world on the above four pillars of the solidarity of humankind, the unity of all life, the interdependent organic nature of the planet Earth, and the oneness of the Ultimate Reality. These four pillars of an Integrated World Order are also inspired by the important lessons learned from the crises facing the world and the COVID-19 pandemic as outlined in chapters 1 &2 above.

Protecting the environmental health and ecological harmony of Mother Earth, and promoting the social, economic, political, religious and technological wellbeing of humankind constitute the two-fold Collective Eco-Spiritual Responsibility entrusted to all peace-loving people of goodwill in the pandemic-devastated world today.

The healthy, peaceful and happy coexistence of humankind on planet Earth will depend upon the seriousness and sincerity with which we adopt and promote this much-needed Collective Eco-Spiritual Responsibility entrusted to us by history and destiny.

A culture of love, peace and sustainable development in the pandemic-devastated world can emerge only if a critical percentage of the human race adopt and promote the concept of 'Collective Eco-Spiritual Responsibility' in their own lives. For this, we will have to develop an abiding unity of spirit and purpose among individuals, families, communities, nations, and religions on earth. We will also have to live in harmony with Mother Nature and with all other species of living beings inhabiting our Common

Planetary Home. This will need an abiding 'Unitive Eco-Spiritual Consciousness' inspired by the spiritual unity underlying the immense physical diversity seen in the material world. Developing such an all-embracing 'Unitive Eco-Spiritual Consciousness' (UESC) within and among people in the pandemic-devastated world is an urgent and important task ahead of humanity if it is to succeed in establishing a culture of love, peace and sustainable development on earth.

An abiding Unitive Eco-Spiritual Consciousness inspired by the spiritual unity underlying the physical diversities in the world is an essential requirement for the emergence of a culture of love, peace and sustainable development in the pandemic-devastated world. This in turn will need an effective spiritual exercise in the form of a meditation which can expand our consciousness to a level of maturity when we can accept our Collective Eco-Spiritual Responsibility willingly and consciously.

Forgiveness, reconciliation, gratitude and self-surrender constitute the four 'pillars' of an abiding Unitive Eco-Spiritual Consciousness without which the much-needed Collective Eco-Spiritual Responsibility cannot be developed. These are also the four pillars of a 'fruitful life' in this world. The term 'fruitful life' implies a peaceful, prosperous, happy, creative and productive life lived with joy and gratitude for the common good of all.

The World Health Organization has pointed out that more than 60% of the sicknesses suffered by humankind in the modern world are psychosomatic in their origins. Learned medical doctors and enlightened spiritual masters have also pointed out that forgiveness and reconciliation are the two most important requirements for physical, mental and spiritual health. They have also discovered and taught us that an 'attitude of gratitude' to everyone and for everything, and a willing and joyful 'self-surrender' to Divine

Providence are also two very essential requirements for physical, mental and spiritual health.

Over the years of our *sadhana* and *tapasya,* we have developed an Inner Peace Meditation termed 'Shanti Yajna' for improving one's physical, mental and spiritual health based on the four socio-spiritual pillars of forgiveness, reconciliation, gratitude and self-surrender. The Shanti Yajna Meditation is more popularly known as 'Peace of Christ Meditation' because the socio-spiritual 'gifts' of forgiveness, reconciliation, gratitude and self-surrender we have received from the eternally loving and ever-compassionate Parent God in, with, and through the Christ-Spirit. It is also known as 'New Creation Meditation', because it can help to make us 'new creations' in Christ through forgiveness, reconciliation, gratitude and self-surrender.

'Christ-Spirit' is the Spirit of forgiveness, reconciliation, gratitude, and self-surrender given to humanity by the Divine Providence in, with, and through Sadguru Jesus Christ.

Just as one need not become a British citizen to listen to BBC News, one also need not become a 'baptized' Christian to receive the Christ-Spirit of forgiveness, reconciliation, gratitude and self-surrender. All people of goodwill can receive the Christ-Spirit by willingly and consciously accepting Sadguru Jesus Christ as the Lord and Master of their hearts and lives. I have experienced this truth in my own life.

There is also no need for any religious conversion or cultural alienation for practicing the Peace of Christ Meditation which will develop in us a Unitive Eco-Spiritual Consciousness. The Unitive Eco-Spiritual Consciousness in turn will develop in us the much-needed Collective Eco-Spiritual Responsibility that will motivate us to accept and fulfill our responsibility to rebuild the pandemic-devastated and violence-ridden world on the strong foundation of an eco-spiritual peace and sustainable development paradigm based on the 'Indian face of the Christian faith' presented in the following Part-Two of this book.

PART TWO

AN INDIAN FACE
OF THE CHRISTIAN FAITH

Introduction ... 69

Constituent – 1   The Unbound Christ ... 72

Constituent – 2   Open Christianity ... 75

Constituent – 3   The Interreligious Theology ... 82

Constituent – 4   Advaitic Christology ... 93

Constituent – 5   Inclusive Missiology ... 98

Constituent – 6   Liberative Spirituality ... 103

Constituent – 7   Holistic Philosophy ... 119

Constituent – 8   Eco-Spiritual Ideology ... 132

Constituent – 9   Enlightened Christian Leadership ... 143

Constituent – 10   Christian Mission Methodologies ... 149

Constituent – 11   The Peace of Christ Meditation ... 155

Constituent – 12   Fruitful Christian Life ... 159

'Dharma Bharathi Darsana Samhita' ... 162

The Tree of *'Dharma Bharathi'* ... 165

Introduction

We have seen in chapter-3, Part-One that India and the Indian Church have important roles to play in rebuilding the pandemic-devastated world. However, in order to be effective in her divine mission, India will have to rediscover her own rich and universal eco-spiritual roots and rebuild herself upon them. A peace and sustainable development paradigm based on a scientific Unitive Eco-Spiritual Consciousness will be India's greatest contribution to humanity. It is also an urgent need of the era for developing an Integrated World Order.

India urgently needs an Integral Renaissance to bring about a moral and spiritual regeneration of the social, economic, political, religious and ecological dimensions of her national life. This is an important requirement for enabling India to play her destined role in the world family of nations. In the multi-religious context of India, this will be an interreligious task. The Indian Church has an important and historic role to play in bringing about this Integral Renaissance of India through interreligious cooperative action.

In order to be fully Indian and fully Christian, the Indian Church will have to make her own the mission of transforming the pandemic-devastated world into a 'New Creation in Christ' based on an 'Indian face of the Christian faith'. This divine mission has to begin from and with India itself. An Integral Renaissance of India is a historic imperative for transforming India into a New Creation in Christ. Only then can the vision and mission of the Indian Church and the Indian Republic be fully harmonized with the vision and mission of the Kingdom of God on earth.

The living Spirit of Christ will have to provide the 'soul force' to the Integral Renaissance of India. This will first of all require an 'Indian face of the Christian faith' inspired by the concepts of 'creative fidelity' and 'collective eco-spiritual responsibility' as outlined in chapters 5 & 6 of Part-One. Developing and promoting such an 'Indian face of the Christian faith' without religious conversion and cultural alienation is the divine mission entrusted to the disciples of Sadguru Jesus Christ in India today.

*   *   *   *   *   *   *   *

The twelve important Constituents of the 'Indian face of the Christian faith' developed during the last four decades (beginning with my personal experience of the infinite love and abiding grace of God in, with and through a serious air accident in July 1982 while serving as an officer in the Indian Air Force) are presented in the following 12 chapters. These 12 Constituents of the 'Indian face of the Christian faith' are:

Constituent-1: Unbound Christ

Constituent-2: Open Christianity

Constituent-3: Interreligious Theology

Constituent-4: Advaitic Christology

Constituent-5: Inclusive Missiology

Constituent-6: Liberative Spirituality

Constituent-7: Holistic Philosophy

Constituent-8: Eco-Spiritual Ideology

Constituent-9: Enlightened Christian Leadership

Constituent-10: Christian Mission Methodologies

Constituent-11: Peace of Christ Meditation

Constituent-12: Fruitful Christian Life

These 12 Constituents themselves are summaries of what were written earlier on these themes in my following 10 books:

1. 'A Vision and a Mission for the Third Millennium' (2005)

2. 'An Indian Face of the Christian Faith' (2009)

3. 'The Second Freedom Struggle of India' (2013)

4. 'Kingdom of God Through Sahana Yoga' (2013)

5. 'Integral Revolution' (2015)

6. 'The Air Plot' (2017)

7. 'Bharatiya Dharma Rajya: Vision of Kingdom of God in India' (2018)

8. 'A New Vision of Christianity' (2018)

9. 'A New Creation in Christ' (2020)

10. 'Viswa Shanti Peetam' (2021)

The twelve Constituents of the 'Indian face of the Christian faith' together form a new 'School of Thought' termed *Dharma Bharathi* School of Thought or *'Dharma Bharathi Darsana Samhita'*.

The twelve Constituents of *'Dharma Bharathi Darsana Samhita'* are briefly explained in the following 12 chapters.

Constituent – 1

The Unbound Christ

The term 'Unbound Christ' implies the 'Word of God' that existed before creation. This Word was with God and was God. All things are created through this Word (John 1: 1-3). This 'Word of God' is present in all Religions and Scriptures of humankind in varying degrees and measures.

Jesus of Nazareth was the perfect Incarnation of the Word of God in human history. His disciples identified him as 'Christ, the Son of the living God' (Matt 16: 16). However, the Word of God cannot be limited to the historical person of Jesus of Nazareth alone. Such a claim will be a metaphysical blunder. He is 'the way, the truth, and the life' in humanity's quest for God (John 14: 6).

Christianity and other religions of humankind and their Scriptures at their best can only be 'pointers' and 'witnesses' to God and to the Word of God. None of them can claim any monopoly over God or the Word of God. Pride, ignorance, selfishness, superstitions, arrogance and smallness of mind are behind all such claims.

Christianity by virtue of being founded on the faith in the Word of God incarnated in, with, and through Lord Jesus Christ, has a very important role to play and a great responsibility to fulfill in helping humanity to come to a deeper understanding and experience of the one true God through the Word of God incarnated in, with and through Lord Jesus Christ.

Lord Jesus Christ is not the 'Founder' of Christianity, but he is the 'Foundation' of Christianity. This also makes Christianity quite different from all other religions of the world. It also calls Christianity to be the power and wisdom of God ever active in the world for ushering in the Kingdom of God on earth because Christ is the power and wisdom of God. (1 Cor 1: 24).

Knowing the 'one true God and Jesus Christ whom He has sent' is the basis and prerequisite of 'eternal life' as taught by the Divine Master (John 17: 3) whom the Christians of all Churches and denominations claim to follow and worship.

The knowledge of the one true God and His Word is not confined to or bound with Christianity and the Holy Bible alone. Other Religions and their Scriptures are also pointers to and custodians of such a redemptive knowledge of the one true God and His 'Unbound Christ'. All that is needed to understand this truth is to develop a 'Christ-Consciousness'.

By the term 'Christ-Consciousness' we mean that divine Consciousness which had incarnated in the person of Lord Jesus Christ, and which enabled him to live and work in this world with such deep and abiding love for God and humanity. It is that consciousness which enabled the Divine Master to accept willingly the suffering death on the cross by submitting himself fully and unconditionally to the 'Will' of God, whom he had addressed as 'Our Father in Heaven' (Matt 6: 9).

Lord Jesus Christ had an intimate personal relationship with God as a beloved son with his ever loving and infinitely forgiving merciful father. He was 'the beloved Son, with whom God was well pleased' (Matt 3: 17). He also enjoyed the status of being the *"only begotten Son, that whoever believes in him should not perish but have everlasting life"* (John 3: 16).

The Christ-Consciousness is also being referred to by us as 'Unitive Eco-Spiritual Consciousness' which will enable us to see the spiritual unity underlying all apparent physical diversities in the world.

Unitive Eco-Spiritual Consciousness will also help us to understand the all-pervasive nature of God, the solidarity of humankind, the unity of all life, and the interdependent organic nature of Planet Earth. It will further enable us to experience the truth of the dictum, 'God in All & All in God'. (Please ref. chapter-6, Part-One). The departing prayer of Lord Jesus Christ was for an abiding unity among all his disciples and among all those people of goodwill who believed in him (John 17: 20-26).

Through the Christ-Consciousness, we will also come to experience the truth of the biblical revelation, *'we live, move, and have our being in God'* (Acts 17: 28). It is upon the strong and deep foundation of such a Christ- Consciousness that humanity is called to build its future.

An Integrated World Order built on the strong foundation of a Unitive Eco-Spiritual Consciousness/Christ Consciousness alone can withstand the trials and tribulations of history, and usher in a culture of abiding peace and sustainable development on earth. This will in turn provide a strong socio-spiritual foundation for the Kingdom of God/ 'Government of God' on earth.

Constituent – 2

Open Christianity

The term 'Open Christianity' implies a way of life rooted in Christ-Consciousness and guided by the teachings of Lord Jesus Christ as recorded in the four Gospels, especially in the 'Sermon on the Mount' (Matt 5, 6 & 7). The corner stone and source of strength of this Open Christianity is a living and loving relationship with the person of the crucified and risen Lord who is the same yesterday, today, and forever (Heb 13: 8).

'Open Christianity' also implies living one's life inspired and guided by the Christ-Consciousness dwelling within the 'cave' of one's heart, in the depths of one's own being.

All peace-loving people of goodwill in the world, irrespective of their religious, cultural, linguistic, geographical, ideological, ethnic and gender differences, can live happy and fruitful lives based on the concept of Open Christianity, and be enriched and enlightened by it. The various Christian Churches in the pandemic-devastated world, are to be seen as various autonomous communities of people of goodwill living this Open Christianity in their own time-space contexts, united to one another with an abiding love as embodied and exemplified by their Divine Master (John 13: 34-35 & John

15: 12 -13) and guided by his teachings that are reminded and clarified to his disciples by the Holy Spirit.

The various Christian Churches/Communities in the world may have different ritualistic, doctrinal, sacramental, physical and cultural expressions given to their Christian faith from time to time and from place to place. But all of them share the same spiritual experience of the one true God, and His Word-Incarnate in Jesus of Nazareth the Christ.

The Open Christianity will be like a large tree with many branches. It is the vision of a Global Ecumenical Church inspired by an Unbound Christ and rooted in the Christ-Consciousness. Every Christian Church/Community in the world will be seen as an important and unique organ of this 'Mystical Body' of Christ, the Global Ecumenical Church, with a specific and unique function to perform in the world.

Every disciple of Lord Jesus Christ and every Christian Church will be an important constituent of the 'Mystical Body' of Christ. But they can remain so only as long as they are united to one another through an abiding love inspired by the Christ-Consciousness, and are guided by the teachings of Lord Jesus Christ. "By this, all will know that you are my disciples, if you have love for one another" (John 13: 35). Unity among his disciples was the prayer of the Lord (John 17: 21).

Many Christians and Christian Churches in India today tarnish the image of Christ by their unethical and immoral lives. As Swami Vivekananda had pointed out more than a century ago, 'more people are alienated from Christ in India by Christians preaching Christianity without practicing the Christian values' than by all other forces opposing Christianity in India put together. This brand of hypocritical Christianity must die, so that an authentic

Christianity built on the strong foundations of an Unbound Christ and Open Christianity can emerge.

Just as the institutionalization of Christianity had begun from the West with Rome as its center, the spiritualization of Christianity must begin from the East with India as its center. Within India itself, it is Kerala, the cradle of Christian faith in the Indian sub-continent, that has to be the seedbed and role model of the Indian face of the Christian faith in the pandemic-devastated world. The troubles and tribulations facing the Christian Churches in Kerala today are preludes and prerequisites for the much-needed death and resurrection of these Churches. A new vision of Christianity is impatient to be born for Kerala and India.

We can see Kerala as a 'Second Israel'. The first Israel had given to the pre-pandemic world the crucified and risen Lord, the Redeemer of humanity from sins and sinful forces and structures. The redemptive Gospel of this crucified and risen Lord has been stifled by the widespread immorality and spiritual apathy that have come to afflict the various Christian Churches in the world today. Kerala, the 'Second Israel' has to give to the pandemic-devastated world the *Gospel of abundant life and abiding peace of the risen Christ, the living Lord*. This message of abundant life and abiding peace of the risen Christ will have to break through the cacophony of institutionalized 'Churchianity' and rebuild the Indian Church on the strong foundations of the Unbound Christ and Open Christianity.

A. The Fivefold Paradigm Shifts

In order to develop an 'Indian face of the Christian faith' based on the concept of 'Open Christianity', the disciples of Christ in India will have to undergo the following five essential paradigm shifts in their own individual and collective lives.

1. *A paradigm shift from membership of the Church to discipleship of Christ:* 'Discipleship' is at the core and center of the cultural, religious, and spiritual traditions in India. The term 'Upanishad' implies wisdom imparted by the guru to his disciples sitting at his/her feet. It is by surrendering to a guru that we can learn self-surrender to the Lord. 'Guru' is the one who can remove the darkness of ego and bring divine light into one's life. The Indian Church urgently needs 'Christian gurus' who can bring the light of Christ into the hearts and minds of their disciples by being the 'light of the world' themselves as urged by their Divine Master (Matt 5: 14).

2. *A paradigm shift from loud vocal prayer to silent contemplative prayer:* The sound and fury of many Christian prayer groups are disturbing and repulsive to the people living around them, adding further to the ever-increasing noise pollution. Lord Jesus Christ had taught His disciples to pray silently behind closed doors (Matt 6: 6). Contemplative prayer awakens the heart to the indwelling presence of the living Spirit of Christ within 'the cave' of one's heart.

3. *A paradigm shift from 'repetitive loyalty' to the Word of God to 'creative fidelity' to the Spirit of God:* 'Repetitive loyalty' implies repeating verbatim what is written in the Bible or taught by the teachers/leaders of one's Church. It may not open one's heart and mind to the work of the Holy Spirit or to the deeper spiritual meanings of the Word of God in the Scripture or taught by the teacher as it does not use one's own God-given faculties of intellect, imagination and creativity. 'Creative fidelity' implies reinterpreting the written or spoken words to understand the spiritual essence of the words spoken or the lessons taught by the teacher/leader according to the time and context of one's

life and work/mission. It implies being ever guided by the Holy Spirit (John 14: 26).

4. *A paradigm shift from preaching the Gospel to building up the 'Kingdom of God':* Preaching the Gospel and converting people to Christianity is not what is really required today. We need to work together with all peace-loving people of goodwill to build the 'Kingdom of God' (Dharma Rajya) of love, righteousness, peace and reconciliation on earth. This we will have to do in collaboration with all peace-loving people of goodwill belonging to the different religious traditions (and also to no religious traditions) of humankind without religious conversion and cultural alienation.

5. *A paradigm shift from the self-centeredness to other-centeredness:* The consumerist culture of competition and the divisive materialistic philosophy of 'success' are 'self-centered'. We need today an 'other-centered' socio-spiritual culture of cooperation, and a holistic socio-spiritual philosophy of 'fruitfulness'. Consumerism and materialism are the enemies of authentic spirituality. They block our spiritual development. To be 'fruitful' implies to be caring, loving and giving. Authentic spirituality should enable us to become fruitful people.

With these fivefold paradigm shifts in their individual and collective lives, the disciples of the Divine Master in the pandemic-devastated India will also be able to overcome the moral decay and spiritual apathy that have afflicted their individual and collective lives.

Such a fivefold paradigm shift will lay a strong foundation for developing and promoting an Indian face of the Christian faith without religious conversion and cultural alienation.

B.   The Seven Millennial Insights

The Indian face of the Christian faith will have to be further strengthened by an adherence to the following seven millennial insights (insights for the third millennium):

1.   A living and loving communion with God our Heavenly Parent in, with, and through the living Spirit of the crucified and risen Lord Jesus Christ alone will be able to quench the spiritual thirst of authentic Christian seekers for Truth and God in the third millennium.

2.   True disciples of Lord Jesus Christ in the third millennium will have to be interreligious persons of love, righteousness, peace and reconciliation, respecting and accepting with joy and gratitude all that is true, good and beautiful in other religious and cultural traditions of humankind.

3.   Authentic disciples of Lord Jesus Christ in the third millennium will have to be socio-political and eco-spiritual persons committed to social & economic justice, to value-based politics & good governance, and to ecological harmony & environmental health inspired by a Unitive Eco-Spiritual Consciousness which will enable them to see God in all and all in God, and to understand the solidarity of humankind, the unity of all life and the interdependent organic nature of planet Earth.

4.   Interreligious dialogue and cooperative action in the third millennium will have to be based on a Unitive Eco-Spiritual Consciousness inspired by the oneness of the Ultimate Reality, the one true God.

5.   More and more people in the world will be inspired to adopt simple and eco-friendly life-styles with vegetarian food habits in the third millennium.

6. 'Consecrated life' in the third millennium will be open, inter-congregational, inter-denominational, and interreligious without gender discriminations.

7. Being and becoming a New Creation in Christ through deepened meditation and contemplative prayer rooted in the Christ Spirit & Christ Consciousness will be the unique hallmarks of Christian discipleship in the third millennium.

Disciples of Lord Jesus Christ in the pandemic-devastated India will have to prayerfully strive to become New Creations in Christ inspired by the seven millennial insights presented above.

Constituent – 3

The Interreligious Theology

The term 'Theology' here implies study of the Ultimate Reality, God, and His relation to the world and humanity. This is the highest knowledge humanity can ever have. All other fields and forms of knowledge find their meanings, places and roles in relation to this Ultimate knowledge. Hence, a correct knowledge of God is of the greatest importance for humankind.

'Know God, know peace. No God, no peace'. This dictum motivated me to launch out on a sincere quest to know the one true God. Knowing the one true God is an essential prerequisite for anyone who is called to be an effective instrument of peace. Hence, a quest to know God has been my most important spiritual quest.

The God we worship will also determine our worldview, character, relationships, value system, and attitude. Hence, it is very important for us to have a right insight into and a clear understanding of the nature of the one true God. Every great religious or spiritual movement in human history had begun with a new knowledge of the Ultimate Reality, God.

Our ability to understand the nature of the one true God will depend on the level to which our consciousness has evolved and our vision has expanded. As we grow in wisdom and consciousness, our understanding of the one true God and His attributes also keep changing.

God has no gender and is the omnipotent, omnipresent, and omniscient Supreme Spirit. But for easy reference, following the Christian tradition in which I was born and brought up, I have been using masculine gender to refer to God all through this book.

Given below are my insights and understanding of God gained from my four gurus, from the four religions in which I have lived-life experiences and from my own personal reflections and experiences. These have been centered on Sadguru Jesus Christ and guided by his living Spirit.

God is 'One in All & All in One' and is the Supreme Spirit beyond all names, forms, and attributes. God manifests Himself through the creation which is His Self-expression bound with time and space. Creation is complete in God but unfolds in time and space. Out of the scientific discoveries about the origin of the universe, my insights and convictions are closer to the 'Big Bang' theory.

God also expresses Himself more intimately through Scriptures and enlightened saints of various religions. Above all, He expresses Himself through the 'spirit' of every human being and through the 'inner voice' speaking within every human heart and the 'inner light' shining within every human soul.

The one true God, the Ultimate Reality, is the source and goal of human life. He is also the deepest 'meeting point' of religions. All religions have unique, but partial insights into the nature of the one true God. These unique, yet partial understandings of the one true God shared by the different religious traditions of humankind can together provide a deeper and broader understanding of the

Ultimate Reality which is beyond all human imagination and is without any names, forms, and attributes.

God is one, but religions are many. *'Ekam Sat Vipra Bahudha Vadanti'* (Truth is one, but wise men speak of it in various terms) was the insight of the enlightened saints and sages of ancient India. Different religious traditions attribute different qualities, names and forms to the one true God depending upon the levels of the consciousness of their founders and the needs of the people of their times. My lived-life experiences within four religious traditions (Christianity, Hinduism, Islam, and Sikhism) have revealed to me these truths.

An integral understanding of the one true God whose living Spirit is ever active in all religious traditions of humankind is the need of the era. Interreligious harmony and abiding global peace will need such an integral understanding of the one true God.

The vision and nature of God revealed to humanity by Sadguru Jesus Christ who has been my Divine Master and guiding light is: *"God is Spirit, and those who worship him must worship in spirit and truth"* (Jn 4:24). This God who is Spirit also reveals Himself to humanity as a 'Heavenly Father' who is an ocean of Divine Love. Infinite compassion and boundless mercy are the two attributes of this Divine Love that is ever-forgiving, ever-enduring and ever self-giving. Hence, a vision of the one true God implies a personal experience of this ever-forgiving, ever-enduring and ever self-giving love of God in one's own life. Such a personal experience of the Divine Love is the source of abiding peace and true happiness in one's own life and in the world as I have come to understand and experience them in my life.

It is by knowing God that we can know everything else. Knowledge of the Creator is the best way to know the Creation.

The enlightened saints and sages of India had pointed out to us that '*Brahma Vidya*' (knowledge of God) is the greatest knowledge. India has been a land that sought God and Truth incessantly from the beginning of history.

The dictum 'Know God, know peace. No God, no peace', also helped me to understand the importance of knowing the one true God if one is to experience true and abiding peace. I also came to realize that peace in the world is impossible without peace among religions in the world. A shared understanding and experience of the one true God among religions is the deepest foundation for abiding peace among religions in the world.

The inspirations from my four gurus and my journey through the four world religions as well as my many experimental initiatives and the visions I was blessed with, helped me to gain valuable insights into the nature of the one true God. I believe that if these valuable insights can be integrated into a shared common vision of the one true God, it will constitute an Interreligious Theology which will be able to provide a deep and abiding foundation for interreligious harmony and for a culture of abiding peace in the world. I have developed a '*Prabhu Parameshwar*' Theology from my experiences, inspirations, visions, and from the insights gained from my journey through the four theistic religions.

The term '*Parameshwar*' implies the 'Supreme God' or Godhead. '*Prabhu*' implies 'my Lord'. The Supreme God is addressed by us as '*Prabhu Parameshwar*' (my Lord, the Supreme God) with great reverence and devotion.

The *Prabhu Parameshwar* Theology is the most important fruit of my spiritual quest. It is also my unique contribution towards a culture of abiding peace among religions. I have come to this experiential theology in, with, and through the living Spirit of Christ, the crucified and risen Lord.

Any great spiritual awakening and moral regeneration of individuals and communities are always associated with a new insight and deepened experience of the Ultimate Reality, the one true God. The eternal quest of humanity has been to gain ever deeper knowledge of this one true God. Human understanding and experience of the one true God is an ever evolving, ever deepening and ever expanding reality. It changes, and has to change, as we grow in wisdom and as our consciousness is expanded.

The living Spirit of Christ, the Holy Spirit, will lead us to ever deeper and broader understanding of Truth and God. This is the function of the Holy Spirit, which is the gift of God given to humankind through Sadguru Jesus Christ (Jn 14:26). The Holy Spirit is a Christ-like Spirit.

The one true God is the Lord and Source of all Creation. We know very little about our own galaxy, the Milky Way; leave alone the whole Creation. Hence, our knowledge of the Lord and Source of all Creation is also very limited. However, God in His infinite love, compassion, and mercy draws us to Himself through insights and experiences that He grants to us from time to time directly or through different prophets, saints, and scriptures.

One has to be very humble when speaking about God and Creation. Exclusive claims about God, Creation, Truth, Grace, Salvation etc. only show our ignorance and pride, which are the biggest blocks in the path of spiritual growth. One great humiliating experience gained by the modern man from the COVID-19 pandemic is the experience of his insignificance and powerlessness. This has made us humans humbler than ever before.

My spiritual quest for God was deeply inspired by the words of Lord Jesus Christ, *'Eternal life is knowing the one true God and Jesus Christ whom He has sent'* (Jn 17: 3). My pilgrimage of faith has been centered mainly on a quest to know the one true God and the Christ He has sent. The 'starting point' of my pilgrimage of faith was a personal encounter with the living Spirit of Christ at the Air Force Hospital, Bengaluru, soon after my air accident in 1982. It is in, with, and through the living Spirit of Christ that I have gained the vision and experience of the one true God. My lived-life experiences in the four religious traditions have only authenticated and strengthened my theological insights and convictions. In the vision of the one true God presented below as a Triune Reality, the Christian faith in the one true God as a Holy Trinity of 'Father-Son-Holy Spirit' and the Indian experience of the one true God as *'Sat-Chit-Ananda'* are integrated into one Ultimate Reality which we have termed *'Prabhu Parameshwar'*.

*   *   *   *   *   *   *   *

The *Prabhu Parameshwar* Theology has its roots in the four theistic religions and their scriptures through which I had undertaken a spiritual journey. It is a triune theology that presents the Godhead as a Light-Love-Spirit Reality.

I have also used the terms *Sadguru, Satchitanada* and *Paramatman* to represent the Divine Light, Divine Love and Divine Spirit that constitute this Interreligious Theology which is briefly explained below.

1.   God is Light (1 Jn 1: 5)

The one true God is the 'Divine Light' that is the source of all wisdom and enlightenment. It is the Divine Light through which we see everything else. This Divine Light is that 'Great Light beyond all the worlds' as pointed out in Chandogya Upanishad. It is the 'Light of lights' as mentioned in the Guru Grandh Sahib. This Divine Light is also the 'Allah' who is the 'Light of the world' as mentioned in the Holy Quran. It is 'the light that shines on all humankind and enlightens every human soul' as stated in the Gospel according to St. John in the Holy Bible.

All scriptures and religions have within them this Divine Light shining forth in various degrees and measures. This Divine Light awakens all human beings to their divine nature and potential. It empowers us to be the 'light of the world'.

Saints and sages of all religions are often depicted with a halo around their heads. This shows the Divine Light shining upon them and shining forth from within them.

The Divine Light incarnates in all human hearts and minds as 'Universal Wisdom' and as the 'voice of conscience' that speaks to us through the ever small 'inner voice'. This Divine Light also manifests in the form of the eternal 'Sadguru' who ever remains within us as the 'Spirit of truth'. It is the living Spirit of Christ as manifested in Jesus of Nazareth, the Christ.

The indwelling 'Sadguru' leads us from falsehood to truth, from darkness to light and from death to eternal life. We need to be ever united to the living Spirit of the indwelling Sadguru.

The living Spirit of the Sadguru is ever active in the hearts of all. But only those who have learnt to listen to this 'ever small' inner voice alone can feel the presence of the Sadguru-Spirit. We will need a contemplative life of inner silence to be attentive to this inner voice. For this we have to practice meditation regularly. It is in the silence of mind that we can hear the voice of God, and it is in the purity of heart that we can see the face of God.

2.   God is Love (1 Jn. 4:8)

The one true God is also the 'Divine Love' that is the source of all creation and ground of all existence.

'God is love' is a common insight of all religions and a common experience of saints and sages of all religious traditions. Those who love, live in God and become the 'salt of the earth' and 'light of the world'. 'Kingdom of God' implies a world of love. It begins within a loving heart. It is within and among us.

'Heaven' is love-filled existence. 'Hell' is a loveless state. Both heaven and hell are within and among us, here and now. They are our own creations. Infinite mercy and eternal compassion are two attributes of the Divine Love that dwells in every human heart as 'Sat-Chit-Ananda', as Being-Consciousness-Bliss. This realization liberates us from all fears and worries, and sets us joyfully free to be 'gods'.

The Divine Love enables us to forgive and reconcile, and to become instruments of love and peace as well as channels of mercy and compassion in the world, and thus to fulfill the purpose of life on the earth.

The Divine Love is ever forgiving, eternally enduring and totally self-giving. There is no place for 'damnation', 'judgment' and 'eternal hell' in the Divine Love. These are mostly inventions of religions for keeping their followers obedient to their dogmas and doctrines, and subservient to their leadership.

An experience of the Divine Love in the depth of our own being awakens us to our inherent divinity. This self-knowledge of oneself as 'god' is a liberating and elevating experience.

The Divine Love also has within it the spirit of healing and reconciliation, and the spirit of dynamism and creativity.

Mother, father and teacher are the first and most important 'divine instruments' through whom we, human beings, experience the Divine Love in our lives. They are the 'channels of divine grace' in one's life. Hence, they are to be respected and served with love and gratitude.

A society where parents and teachers are not respected and served with love and gratitude, and a society where the parents and teachers themselves are not fulfilling their divinely ordained responsibilities with love, will surely fall into spiritual apathy and moral decay. A spiritual and moral regeneration of any society has to begin with a spiritual and moral regeneration of the parents and teachers, especially the mothers, in that society.

A renewed love and an increased respect for parents and teachers will also be essential for the spiritual and moral regeneration of a society. The selfless love within one's own heart is the true measure of the divinity within oneself. We become divine to the extent we are able to love others selflessly.

All religions and their scriptures are meant to help their followers to become more divine with hearts filled with ever greater measures of selfless love.

3.   God is Spirit (Jn 4: 24)

The one true God is also the omnipotent, omniscient, and omnipresent 'Supreme Spirit', the *Paramatman,* beyond all names, forms, and attributes in whom the whole creation has its very existence. 'God is Spirit', taught Sadguru Jesus Christ (Jn 4:24). The Upanishads speak of God as Consciousness. '*Pragyanam Brahman*' (God is Consciousness), says the Aitareya Upanishad. This Supreme Spirit/Consciousness is the Source of all energy and power, and of all life and being. We live, move, and have our being in this Supreme Spirit/Consciousness.

The Divine Spirit is the Source of the Divine Light and the Divine Love. This Supreme Spirit is omnipotent, omniscient, and omnipresent. It is the Source and Ground of all existence. It is the Source of all power and wisdom.

The Supreme Spirit permeates and enlivens the whole Creation. It is also the Source of all intellect, imagination and creativity.

The human spirit, the *'Atman'*, is the image and likeness of the *Paramatman,* the Supreme Spirit. Hence, we can say that 'human beings are created in the image and likeness of God.'

We are spiritual beings in physical bodies. The body is temporal. It is subject to decay and death. The spirit is eternal. It does not decay or die. It is beyond all time-space limitations. We are children of eternity, *'Amrutasyaputrah'*. We are 'gods' within the one true God. We need to keep this truth always in mind and be free from all fear, worry, and tension.

God, the Ultimate Reality, is Spirit and Energy beyond names and forms. This is a truth accepted not only by most of the religions, but also by many scientists all over the world who do not follow any religion.

The triune vision of the one true God presented above is termed *'Prabhu Parameshwar'* by us for easy identification. The one true God, *Prabhu Parameshwar,* is a Divine Trinity (*Ishwariya Trayam*) of Divine Light – Divine Love – Divine Spirit, of *Sadguru-Satchitananda-Paramatman.* I have come to an experiential knowledge of this one true God by being a disciple of Sadguru Jesus Christ and following the 'Way' of the Divine Love that is ever forgiving, enduring, and self-giving as taught by him. I have accepted him as my 'Divine Master' who has been 'the path, the truth and the life' in my quest for God and eternal life, and in my search for the meaning and purpose of my 'second life' in the multi-religious context of India, where I have been destined to live my physical life.

Lord Jesus Christ is the 'face' of the one true God in human history, and it is only through him that I could have a glimpse of what and who God is like. He is the Incarnation of the Triune God of Light-Love-Spirit. He is the 'light of the world' (Jn 8:12). He is the love of God incarnate (Jn 3:16). The Spirit of God was in him (Jn 2:32-33). Hence, Sadguru Jesus Christ is God incarnate. He is God himself for humankind. He is same yesterday, today, and forever (Hebrews 13:8).

My understanding, experience and vision of the one true God as *Sadguru-Satchitananda-Paramatman* are depicted in and expressed through the Logo given on the back cover of this book.

Constituent – 4

Advaitic Christology

The term 'Christology' implies here the theological interpretation of the person and work of Lord Jesus Christ. 'Advaitic' implies non-dual.

After my first personal encounter with the living Spirit of Christ at the Air Force Hospital, Bengaluru, in 1982, my whole effort was to understand the person of Jesus Christ; praying to Him I had that first encounter. I also recollected my encounter with the evil spirit at Port Blair in 1975 and how the name of Jesus Christ had saved me from it. The deeper I went into this quest of understanding the person of Jesus Christ, the more I realized his divinity.

Jesus of Nazareth was the incarnation of Christ in human history, and Christ was the Word of God. This Word of God was God Himself. *"In the beginning was the Word, and the Word was with God, and the Word was God. All things were made through Him, and without Him nothing was made. In Him was life, and the life was the light of men"* (Jn 1: 1-4). These opening words in the Gospel narrative of Apostle John, the beloved disciple of the Divine Master, authenticated my understanding of Jesus of history and Christ, the Word of God, and their interconnectedness. I came to realize that the historical Jesus of Nazareth was the incarnation of Christ, the eternal Word of God, in human history bound with time and space.

But when I had to share my Christ-experience with my friends and co-workers in India from other religious traditions, I had to use terms and terminologies that could be understood by them. Most of my friends and co-workers, both in the Indian Air Force and outside the Air Force, were from other religious traditions, mostly from the Hindu religious tradition. Hinduism is a very open and liberal religion. I have often referred to it as the 'mother' of all religions. It has different schools of thought (*Darsana*) within it. The 'Advaita' school of thought is by far the most evolved school of thought in Hinduism. Hence, I wanted to develop an authentically Indian 'Advaitic Christology' that could lead my Hindu friends to a deep communion with God through the Christ-Spirit. This search finally led me to develop the 'Sadguru' Christology which has become the foundation of the 'Indian face' of the Christian faith that is being promoted by us today.

> 'Christology' deals with knowledge and experience of the divinity of Christ and its practical applications in our lived-life contexts. I was inspired to develop the 'Sadguru' Christology in the Indian socio-religious context inspired by the qualities and characteristics of the 'Sadguru' that are presented in the following verses from the Viswasara Tantra:

"Brahmanandam paramasukhadam kevalam jnanamoortim;
Dwantateetam gaganasadrushyam tatwamasyadi lakshyam;
Ekam nityam vimalam achalam sarvadim sakshibhutam;
Bhavatitam trigunarahitam Sadgurum tamnamami."

- **Viswasara Tantra**

(Meaning: 'I bow to the True Guru who is the embodiment of the Bliss of God; Who bestows supreme happiness; the Absolute

Who is Wisdom Incarnate; Who is beyond any duality; Who is vast like the sky; Whom 'Thou Art That' and similar Scriptural verses have in view; Who is the One, the Eternal, the Pure, the Immovable, the Witness to all; Who is beyond all *bhavas*, devoid of the three *gunas*'.)

The 'Sadguru' according to this revelation is the True Guru who is none other than the incarnation of God on earth. He alone can lead us from falsehood to truth, from darkness to light and from death to eternal life. Lord Jesus Christ claimed himself to be 'the path, the truth and the life' in humanity's quest for God in this world. 'No one comes to the Father except through me', he told his disciples (Jn 14: 6). I realized that the path of forgiving, enduring, and self-sacrificing love taught by him is the only way to understand and realize the truth of God. I also realized that God is an ocean of infinite love (1 Jn 4: 8) and that the living Spirit of Christ is the Source of life (Jn 1: 4). These revelations motivated me to accept and present Lord Jesus Christ as the 'Sadguru' in humanity's quest for truth, light, and eternal life from an Indian socio-religious perspective.

I have found that many Indians, especially many of the educated Hindus, have no difficulty in accepting Lord Jesus Christ as their Sadguru and in surrendering themselves totally to him. Religious conversion and cultural alienation are not required in this process of master-disciple relationship, which is an integral part of India's religious and spiritual traditions.

However, a *community* of disciples of the Divine Master is essential for its members to grow in God-experience and Christian discipleship. For creating such communities, some kind of social system and symbolism need to be adopted. The Jews had 'circumcision'. Christian Churches have 'baptism'. In the Hindu traditions, we have 'diksha' which is a traditional way of initiating a disciple by the guru. This is more of a spiritual initiation than a 'sacrament' or ritual. This had been the Upanishadic tradition.

The Upanishads are treasure houses of divine wisdom. The term 'Upanishad' itself implies divine wisdom taught by the guru to his disciples sitting at his feet. The disciples were totally surrendered to the guru. The guru also deeply loved his disciples. There was neither religious conversion nor cultural alienation required in such a deep and abiding master-disciple relationship. Sadguru Jesus Christ also claimed himself to be the Teacher and Lord for his disciples (Jn. 13:13). He demanded total loyalty from his disciples (Lk 14: 25-33). He wanted them to be united to him like a branch to the vine (Jn. 15: 1- 5). In turn, he offered himself totally to them. He instituted the 'Lord's Supper' through which the memorial of his total self-giving is commemorated by his disciples all over the world and all through history.

Just as Jesus of Nazareth was presented as the 'Christ' (anointed one of God) from a Greek perspective in the beginning of Christianity, he can very well be presented as the 'Sadguru' from an Indian socio-religious perspective without religious conversion and cultural alienation.

I have also come to realize that the living Spirit of Christ can be expressed and experienced as the 'Sadguru-Spirit' that dwells in all human hearts to guide us in the path of truth, light and eternal life. This has been India's prayer from time immemorial:

'Asathoma Sadgamaya
Tamasoma Jyotirgamaya
Mrityorma Amritamgamaya'   **(Brahadaranyaka Upanishad)**

(Meaning: Lead me from falsehood to truth; Lead me from darkness to light; Lead me from death to eternal life.)

It is the one 'Sadguru-Spirit' who dwells in the hearts of all human persons; more so, in the hearts of all enlightened prophets, saints, and spiritual masters of humankind. In Sadguru Jesus Christ, the Sadguru-Spirit had found its human and historical perfection. Hence, he is the 'standard' and best model of the Sadguru-Spirit/Christ-Spirit present and active in human history.

The Sadguru Christology will liberate Lord Jesus Christ from the bondage of western Christian Churches and present to the world an 'Unbound Christ' and 'Open Christianity' with a liberative spirituality of love as its foundation.

My quest for an 'Advaitic Christology' also resulted in leading me to a deeper understanding of the divinity of Lord Jesus Christ. It also helped me in developing the 'Sadguru' Christology as the foundation of the 'Indian face of the Christian Faith'.

My quest led me to realize that the Sadguru Christology is an Advaitic Chrsitology as well. 'Advaita' implies not two. Neither does it mean one. Sadguru Jesus Christ was intimately related to God the Father, yet he had a distinct identity of his own.

"I am in the Father and the Father is in me" (Jn 14: 11). This was his experience. He prayed that his disciples may also be one with them. *'They all may be one, as you, Father, are in me and I in you'* (Jn 17: 21). This is 'Christian Advaita'. Hence, the Sadguru Christology is also an Advaitic Christology at its best.

Constituent – 5

Inclusive Missiology

The term 'Missiology' implies the study and science of missions. The Missiology offered and promoted by us for the 'Indian face of the Christian faith' is termed *'Dharma Rajya'* Missiology. This is a 'Kingdom of God' Missiology.

A mission needs a vision. The vision is the most important part of any mission. Mission is like the journey and vision is like the destination. No one undertakes a journey without a destination. When the vision and mission are integrated, there will be great 'synergy' (collective spiritual energy). This was the model presented by Sadguru Jesus Christ. 'Kingdom of God' was the vision and mission of the Divine Master. It was a destination as well as a realization. The term 'Kingdom of God' (or 'Kingdom of Heaven') appears more than 100 times in the Gospels. It was the central theme of the life and mission of Sadguru Jesus Christ. It was an all-inclusive vision and mission. It included the whole humankind; sinners and saints; poor and rich; men and women; Jews and the 'gentiles'; black and white, alike. Unfortunately, the many 'Churches' initiated by his self-proclaimed disciples in his name have lost this all-inclusive vision and mission of the 'Kingdom of God' initiated by their Divine Master as they gained wealth, influence and power in the world.

Motivated by a colonial mindset, the westernized Christianity equated the Church with the Kingdom of God and went around preaching this version of Christianity as the only true religion. This also meant converting all others to this 'only true religion' to 'save their souls' from going to 'eternal hell'. The vision and mission initiated by the Divine Master were totally lost to the westernized colonial 'Churchianity'.

Regaining the vision and mission of the Kingdom of God initiated by the Divine Master, and committing themselves wholeheartedly to its realization on earth is the only way in which disciples of Sadguru Jesus Christ can make themselves relevant to their divine call and mission in the present era.

'Peace in the world is impossible without peace among religions in the world'. This is an insight shared by many sincere religious thinkers and theologians in the modern world. Religions need a shared vision and mission if they are to work together. The truth of this discovery can be tested and proved by anyone who is really committed to a mission of peace-building in a multi-religious context.

The vision and mission initiated by Sadguru Jesus Christ in this world was the 'Kingdom of God'. This vision and mission was initiated by him by realizing them first in his own being and life. Love, truth, unity, peace, joy and abundant life were the important constituents of the Kingdom of God realized by him in his own life and being, and promoted by him in the world (John 15:12; 14: 6; 17: 21; 14:27; 15:11 & 10:10). In the socio-religious milieu of India the term closest to 'Kingdom of God' is 'Dharma Rajya'.

The word 'dharma' comes from the Sanskrit root *dhr*, which means to hold together, to unite, or to integrate. Hence, 'dharma' is that which holds together, that which unites, that which integrates.

Love is the foundation of such an abiding unity among people; peace is its fruit. Where there is love, unity and peace, there will also be happiness. Thus, 'dharma' is an integral concept built on the cornerstones of love, unity, peace, and happiness. The concept of 'Dharma' is one of the greatest contributions of India to human thought.

The word 'dharma' is also very often used to mean 'duty' and/or 'righteousness'. It is by fulfilling our duties to our families and to our communities as well as to the nation and humanity at large that we can be instruments of God for building up His Kingdom on earth. It is by righteous conduct (righteousness) that we can establish abiding unity and peace with others in the family, in the society, and in the nation and the world. Peace in one's life and in the family/community/society will remain a mirage without forgiveness and reconciliation. Hence, we can redefine 'Dharma Rajya' as the *Kingdom of God of love, righteousness, peace and reconciliation.'*

The popular use of the word 'Dharma' is in relation to various religions. The English word 'religion' comes from the Latin word *'religare'* which means to unite, to hold together, to bind together. Thus, we have the 'Hindu Dharma' that unites all those who follow Hinduism; the 'Muslim Dharma' that unites all those who follow Islam; the 'Christian Dharma' that unites all those who follow Christianity; the 'Sikh Dharma' that unites all those who follow Sikhism; the 'Buddhist Dharma' that unites all those who follow Buddhism; the 'Jain Dharma' that unites all those who follow Jainism; the 'Baha'i Dharma' that unites all those who follow the Baha'i religion; the 'Jewish Dharma' that unites all those who follow Judaism; the 'Parsi Dharma' that unites all those who follow Zoroastrianism;.... so on and so forth.

The term *'Christu Dharma'* is used by us to imply an 'Open Christianity' based on an 'Unbound Christ'. It can unite the whole humankind in 'Christ-Consciousness'.

The word 'dharma' also has many other applications and connotations. 'Sanatana Dharma' (Eternal Religion) is a term often used for referring to a religious culture that existed in the Indian subcontinent before the emergence of organized religions. 'Swadharma' implies one's duty to one's own self and to one's own near and dear ones. 'Samaj Dharma' implies one's responsibility to one's community/society. 'Rashtra Dharma' means our duties towards our country. 'Manav Dharma' implies one's duty to the human society. 'Yuga Dharma' implies the mission of the era. There can be many more connotations and usages for the word Dharma.

According to Dr. Annie Besant, 'Dharma' is 'India's word to the world'. She had pointed out:

> "When the nations of the world were sent forth one after the other, a special word was given by God to each, the word which each was to say to the world, the peculiar word from the Eternal which each one was to speak. As we glance over the history of the nations, we can hear resounding from the collective mouth of the people this word, spoken out in action, the contribution of that nation to the ideal and perfect humanity. To Egypt in old days, the word was Religion; to Persia the word was Purity, to Chaldea the word was Science, to Greece the word was Beauty, to Rome the word was Law; and to India, the eldest born of His children, He gave the word that summed up the whole in one, the word Dharma. That is the word of India to the world."

Irrespective of the various connotations and usages of the word 'Dharma', there lies at their core an understanding of the abiding spiritual unity behind all apparent physical diversities. Discoveries of modern science also clearly point to this underlying unity and oneness of reality. Love is the basis of unity. Peace and happiness are fruits of love and unity.

In the 'tree of Dharma', love is like the root, unity and righteousness are like the trunk and branches; happiness and peace are like its flowers and fruits.

The concepts of 'Dharma' and 'Dharma Rajya' had their roots deep in the collective psyche of the people of India much before the *'Christu Marga'* (Way of Christ) was brought to this ancient land of religions by Apostle Thomas, a direct disciple of Sadguru Jesus Christ, in 52 AD. The *Christu Marga* helped to make the concepts of 'Dharma' and 'Dharma Rajya' dynamic and creative in the Indian soil by integrating them with the vision and mission of the Kingdom God on earth preached and initiated by Sadguru Jesus Christ.

Christians and Christian Churches today need to rediscover the original vision and mission of Sadguru Jesus Christ and reinterpret them in the multi-religious context of India based on the lessons taught by the COVID-19 pandemic. Disciples of Sadguru Jesus Christ need to be rededicated to God for the very purpose of helping Christians and Christian Churches in India to awaken and empower themselves for fulfilling this divine mission entrusted to them by history and destiny.

In the Indian context of our mission the term *'Bharatiya Dharma Rajya'* is used by us to represent the vision of a spiritually awakened, morally regenerated, economically prosperous and politically strong great new India that will be a land and light of love, righteousness, peace, and reconciliation on earth. Hence, for Christians and Christian Churches in India, working together with all peace-loving people of goodwill from other religious traditions to transform our pandemic-devastated country into a *'Bharatiya Dharma Rajya'* through interreligious dialogue and cooperation will constitute a continuation of the vision and mission of their Divine Master in the pandemic-devastated India.

Constituent – 6

Liberative Spirituality

'Spirituality' is the science of the Spirit. It implies an experiential knowledge of the omnipotent, omnipresent and omniscient Supreme Spirit, the one true God who is the Source of all Being and Ground of all Existence.

'Spirituality' helps to develop an abiding communion of the human spirit with the Divine Spirit. It liberates us from the bondages of the flesh and the world and sets us free to rise to ever higher levels of consciousness. Freedom and love are the experiential aspect of spirituality. True love leads to a great liberative experience. It sets us totally free.

The 'liberative spirituality of love' that is being offered and promoted by us for the 'Indian face of the Christian faith' is termed *'Sahana Yoga'*.

The word *Sahana* implies to suffer, to bear with. *Yoga* implies communion with the Source, with God. God is love. *Sahana* becomes *Yoga* when it is accepted with love for the greater good of oneself and others.

'Sahana Yoga' is defined as *'the spirituality of forgiving, enduring, and self-sacrificing love as it was taught and demonstrated to the*

world by Sadguru Jesus Christ'. The Divine Master is the true guru and the best model of *Sahana Yoga* in human history. The perfection of *Sahana Yoga* is laying down one's life for the good of others with love. Sadguru Jesus Christ taught and demonstrated to the world *Sahana Yoga* at its best. He was the perfect '*Sahana Yogi*' and the greatest teacher of *Sahana Yoga* in human history.

We are inclined to love mostly those who love us. But Sadguru Jesus Christ taught his disciples to love even their enemies and to pray for those who persecuted them. "But I say to you, love your enemies and pray for those who persecute you", he instructed them (Matt 5: 44). He himself demonstrated this to the world by praying for those who crucified him. "Father, forgive them; for they do not know what they are doing" (Luke 23:34), he prayed, rising above the agony of his suffering death on the cross. Thus, Sadguru Jesus Christ became the perfect example and the greatest teacher of *Sahana Yoga* in human history. He is also 'the way, the truth, and the life' (John 14: 6) in humanity's eternal quest for the meaning and purpose of life in this world and thereafter. *Sahana Yoga* is the narrow but sure 'door' and 'path' to eternal life that were revealed, demonstrated and taught to humanity by Sadguru Jesus Christ.

We were taught in the high school that the Metric System of measurement of length and distance is based on a standard 'meter' which is the length of a platinum iridium rod kept in a vacuum tube in a laboratory in Paris. Without such a 'standard meter' serving as its basis, there could not be a Metric System of measurement in the world.

In spiritual matters the guru (master) is always the model and standard for the disciple to learn from and to emulate. The spirit and consciousness of Sadguru Jesus Christ, the Teacher and Lord of *Sahana Yoga,* will provide the source and the divine standard for his disciples in understanding and imbibing this 'Way' at an ever deeper spiritual level.

'Christ-Spirit' is the living Spirit of Christ (Sadguru-Spirit) that had incarnated in the person of Jesus of Nazareth, *the* Christ. 'Christ-Consciousness' is the Unitive Eco-Spiritual Consciousness that had manifested in his life and being. Spirit is the source and ground of Consciousness. Hence, the Christ-Spirit is the source and ground of Christ-Consciousness and hence, of *Sahana Yoga.*

Sadguru Jesus Christ is the divine standard of the Christ-Spirit, Christ-Consciousness and *Sahana Yoga* in human history. He taught the world to "Love one another as I have loved you. No one has greater love than this, to lay down one's life for one's friends" (John 15:12-13). He 'walked the talk' and showed the Way. He himself was the truth of this Way. The living Spirit of Christ gives us the power and wisdom of God to follow this Way of *Sahana Yoga.* The Divine Master also offered 'abundant life' (John 10:10) to all his disciples who dared to follow him by accepting the Way of *Sahana Yoga* offered by him.

a.   Three Constituent Elements of *Sahana Yoga:*

Water is defined as a 'colorless, tasteless, and odorless fluid'. But the constituent elements of water are Hydrogen and Oxygen (H_2O). Similarly, apart from its definition, *Sahana Yoga* also has three constituent elements which can be seen and understood from the lived-life-examples and teachings of Sadguru Jesus Christ, the divine standard and greatest teacher of *Sahana Yoga.*

The Divine Master was ever obedient to the will of God with whom he had a very intimate personal relationship as a beloved son to his ever-loving father. "I have come down from heaven, not to do my own will, but the will of Him who sent me," Sadguru Jesus Christ had pointed out to his disciples (John 6: 38). He also taught his disciples how to pray to God, our 'Heavenly Father' (Matt 6: 9-14). This prayer itself was an act of self-surrender to an ever-loving 'Father in Heaven'.

Total submission and obedience to the Will of God, the Heavenly Father, was the first and most important constituent element of the Christ-Spirit that had manifested in Sadguru Jesus Christ. Hence, it is also the first constituent element of *Sahana Yoga*.

'The Son of Man came to serve, not to be served,' proclaimed Sadguru Jesus Christ about himself. The Divine Master was ever reaching out to the suffering humanity with great love and compassion. His miracles were concrete expressions of his love for the suffering humanity. Those were acts of love flowing out from the divine love and compassion that had filled his Sacred Heart. Anyone whose heart is filled with such divine love and compassion can also perform such 'miracles'. This was yet another truth taught to his disciples by Sadguru Jesus Christ. 'You will do greater things than these,' the Divine Master had assured his disciples (John 14:12). One only has to be filled with great love and compassion. Such divine love is possible only when one is totally surrendered to God, the source and ocean of divine love and compassion, following the example of Sadguru Jesus Christ. Thus, 'selfless service with love' is the second constituent element of *Sahana Yoga* revealed and taught to the world by Sadguru Jesus Christ.

The un-surrendered 'self' or 'ego' can be the greatest obstacle in the path of divine love and compassion. It produces a strong 'I-mine' ego-consciousness and tries to bring the 'self' to the center of our being and life. One who is obsessed with and controlled by the 'self' will not be able to experience the divine love which is always other-centered. Water does not flow upward; it always flows downward, from higher level to lower level. Similarly, the divine love and grace cannot come into a proud and selfish heart. Humility is the basic requirement for purity of heart and for spiritual growth. Humility is developed through humiliations and sufferings. The COVID-19 pandemic has taught us great humility. This is the greatest spiritual contribution of this pandemic.

Divine love and grace can fill our hearts only when the ego- consciousness is sacrificed upon the altar of one's own life following the example of Sadguru Jesus Christ. Sacrificing the ego-consciousness with love for God and fellow human beings is the third constituent element of the Christ-Consciousness, and hence of *Sahana Yoga*.

Thus, submission to the Will of God at all times in all matters, selfless service to the needy fellow human beings, and sacrificing the 'I-mine' ego-consciousness – all done with love – are the three constituent elements of the Christ-Consciousness and therefore of *Sahana Yoga*. Anyone can become a Christ-like person by developing and inculcating the three constituent elements of Christ-Consciousness consisting of submission, service and sacrifice with love in one's own life following the example of Sadguru Jesus Christ. The greater the measure and degree of *Sahana Yoga* in one's life, the more Christ-like a person that he/she can become.

b.   Interreligious nature of *Sahana Yoga:*

The three constituent elements of Christ-Consciousness and *Sahana Yoga* (Submission, Service and Sacrifice with love) are present and active in an integral way in Christianity with Christ at its core and center. But these are also present and active in all religious traditions of the world in varying degrees and measures unique to each of them.

The 'loving surrender' to the Will of God, the 'submission' element of Christ-Consciousness and *Sahana Yoga*, is emphasized in Islam. The very word 'Islam' also implies submission to the Will of God. 'Islam' also means peace. It is through loving submission to the Will of God that we can experience true and lasting peace. This truth is a basic tenet of Islam.

The 'loving service' element of Christ-Consciousness and *Sahana Yoga* is emphasized in Sikhism. *Seva* (service) is one of the important tenets of Sikhism. Every Gurudwara (Sikh temple) has 'Guru-ka-Langar' (free provision of food for all) as an integral part of its worship and service. The 'Guru-ka-Langar' in the Golden Temple at Amritsar is a great wonder by its very magnitude, voluntarism and efficiency. It is a living example of the great importance given to 'Seva' in the Sikh tradition. Sikhism is also a religion of *discipleship*. The word 'Sikh' means disciple. The Sikhs work hard and earn their living with great dignity. They are well known all over the world for their hard work. We will very seldom find a Sikh beggar anywhere in the world. I have not found even one Sikh beggar in my life so far. (I am 74 years of age now) . Sikhs also give generously from the fruits of their labor.

The element of *sacrifice/renunciation* of Christ-Consciousness and *Sahana Yoga* is emphasized in Hinduism, Buddhism and Jainism. These are great religious traditions that emphasize the importance of renunciation and self-sacrifice for spiritual growth and development. The great saints and sages of these religious traditions have been *tyagis* (men and women of renunciation). *Sanyasa* (life of total renunciation) is a socio-religious tradition that is common to Hinduism, Buddhism and Jainism.

Utaracharitanam Tu VasudhaivaKutumbakam (for the noble hearted the whole earth is one family) is the universal vision and wisdom of Hinduism. *Ekam Sat Vipra Bahudhavadanti* (Truth is one, wise men call it by various names), proclaimed the saints and sages of this great religion.

Buddhism is a religion of *Karuna* (compassion). Lord Buddha renounced his royal palace and princely comforts and became a *'bhikku'* (wandering monk) to alleviate the sufferings of the ignorant millions. Buddhism has also developed great meditation techniques to control the mind and its desires which according to Lord Buddha, are at the root of all sufferings. Jainism is a religion of *Ahimsa* (non-violence). It teaches its followers not to harm any living being. The unity and sacredness of all life is a central tenet of Jainism. The Jain *'munis'* (silent saints) are great promoters of peace and non-violence in the world.

The five religions mentioned above do not constitute an exhaustive list. We can also find the elements of the Christ-Consciousness and *Sahana Yoga* in varying degrees and measures in other religious and spiritual traditions of the world as well.

Thus, we can see that the constituent elements of Christ-Consciousness and *Sahana Yoga* are present and working in the different religious traditions of humanity in varying degrees and measures. Understanding this truth and applying it to transform the world into the Kingdom of God built on the pillars of love, righteousness, peace and reconciliation through mutual respect and cooperation based on *Sahana Yoga* is the task ahead of religions and religious leaders in the third millennium. For Christianity and Christian leaders this is also a divine mandate from their Divine Master.

c. Mahavakyas of *Sahana Yoga*

'Mahavakyas' means 'great sayings' that contain great truths. There are four principal *Mahavakyas* in the Vedanta-tradition. They are:

[1] *Pragyanam Brahma* (God is Consciousness - *Aitareya Upanishad* 3.3), [2] *Ayam Atma Brahma* (This Self is Brahman - *Mandukya Upanishad* 1. 2), [3] *Tatvamasi* (You are that - *Chandogya Upansihad*

6. 8. 7), and [4] *Aham Brahmasmi* (I am Divine - *Brihadaranyaka Upanishad* 1.4.10). Other religious scriptures and traditions also have their own great sayings. Similarly, *Sahana Yoga* can also be expressed through three *'Mahavakyas'*.

We have discovered and understood the three constituent elements of Christ-Consciousness and *Sahana Yoga* from the lived-life-examples and teachings of Sadguru Jesus Christ who is the divine standard of *Sahana Yoga*. In the same manner, we can also understand certain redemptive laws and principles of *Sahana Yoga* from his life and teachings. These laws of *Sahana Yoga* are ever active in human history. These eternal laws are termed the *Mahavakyas* of *Sahana Yoga*.

Newton's laws of motion, though they carry the name of Newton, operate independent of Newton. They have a universal validity and application. However, they are applicable only to the physical world, to the world of matter bound with time and space. But the laws of *Sahana Yoga* are operative in, with and through the Christ-Spirit. They are eternal, and are beyond time and space limitations. They are centered on the Christ-Spirit that manifested itself as '*the* path, *the* truth and *the* life' in and through Sadguru Jesus Christ.

Sahana Yoga, when understood well and applied effectively in our spiritual life, can liberate us from all fears of suffering and pain, and even of death. The living Spirit of Christ is ever available to help us in this process. This is the uniqueness of the Christian faith. It is the faith in an ever-living and ever-loving person, Sadguru Jesus Christ, who is same 'yesterday, today and tomorrow', and who is ever available always to help, strengthen, inspire and guide us.

Suffering, especially voluntary suffering for a higher purpose or noble cause, when surrendered to God with love, can lead to purification of one's body and soul, and of one's society. It can also serve as means of redemption for many in the universal body of humanity because every human being is organically and spiritually connected to all other human beings in the larger global family.

The interdependent organic nature of all creation is being proved by the discoveries of modern science today. This insight into the oneness of creation inspired the saints and sages of yore to accept all physical pain and suffering upon their own selves as means for purification and sanctification as well as for redemption of the world. One who has conquered the fear of suffering and death by accepting and integrating the constituent elements of *Sahana Yoga* into his/her life becomes a truly liberated person, *Jeevan Mukta,* following the example of Sadguru Jesus Christ.

Sadguru Jesus Christ became invincible and irresistible through his own victory over death. He suffered unto death on the cross. God raised him from the dead and made him *the* Christ (the anointed one of God) for ever to be the path, truth and life in humanity's eternal quest for liberation (*mukti*) from the bondages of sin, suffering, and death. Thus, *Sahana Yoga* can become the path of liberation (*Mukti Marga*) for ourselves and others if we practice it sincerely and to the best possible extent by following the footstep of Sadguru Jesus Christ, the teacher and lord of *Sahana Yoga.*

'*Sahana Yoga Mukti Marga*' (*Sahana Yoga* is the path of liberation) is thus the first redemptive law of Christ.

Voluntary suffering for the good of others and in communion with others can develop an inner bond between the one voluntarily suffering and the other person for whose sake one has accepted voluntary suffering. The best example is the inner bond between the mother and the child she has delivered through great travail. The sickness and suffering of a dear and near one will bring together relatives and friends around the sickbed. The suffering patient thus becomes a means and source of unity among friends and relatives. Also, natural calamities faced by a community/ city/ country inspire other communities/cities/countries to come for the aid of the one in difficulty. *Sahana Yoga* can thus become a source of unity (*aikya*) among people.

'*Sahana Yoga Aikya Marga*' (*Sahana Yoga* is the path of unity) is thus the second redemptive law of Christ.

Humiliations are painful. But they can help to develop humility in us which is a great spiritual virtue. "Blessed are the poor in spirit, the kingdom of Heaven belongs to them" (Mt. 5:3), taught Sadguru Jesus Christ. This was the first beatitude within his Sermon on the Mount. Poverty of spirit implies humility of character. Humility is an essential requirement for a grace-filled and peaceful life.

A humble person with an 'ethic of enough' enjoys greater peace and happiness than a proud person with great amount of wealth and power.

One who has learnt to accept all sufferings and humiliations with equanimity following the example of Sadguru Jesus Christ is ever at peace with oneself and others. The world cannot give us or take away from us such peace which is beyond human understanding. This is the kind of peace that Sadguru Jesus Christ offers to his disciples who are willing to follow him.

Sahana Yoga is the path of peace (*shanti*). It gives us true and abiding peace which liberates us from all worries and fears.

'*Sahana Yoga Shanti Marga*' (*Sahana Yoga* is the path of peace) is thus the third redemptive law of Christ.

Sahana Yoga Mukti Marga (*Sahana Yoga* is the path of liberation), *Sahana Yoga Aikya Marga* (*Sahana Yoga* is the path of unity), and *Sahana Yoga Shanti Marga* (*Sahana Yoga* is the path of peace) are the three redemptive laws of Christ and of *Sahana Yoga*. We have adopted and presented these as the three *Mahavakyas* of *Sahana Yoga*.

d.   Redemptive applications of *Sahana Yoga*

Based on the three *Mahavakyas*, there are also three important redemptive applications of *Sahana Yoga*:

1. *Liberation:* Liberating oneself and others from injustice, alienation, oppressions, exploitation and forces of sin and evil.

2. *Unity:* Bringing about unity and harmony among people, families, religions and nations.

3. *Peace:* Promoting peace and reconciliation within and among individuals, families, societies, nations and religions in the world.

This three-fold redemptive application of *Sahana Yoga* can be understood from the very mission of Sadguru Jesus Christ as explained by his most ardent disciple, St. Paul, who was specially called and trained by the living Spirit of Christ for a mission to the 'gentile world' of his time. St. Paul wrote to the Ephesians (Eph 2: 14-18):

> *"For he is our peace; in his flesh he has made both groups into one and has broken down the dividing wall, that is, the hostility between us. He has abolished the law with its commandments and ordinances, so that he might create in himself one new humanity in place of the two, thus making peace, and might reconcile both groups to God in one body through the cross, thus putting to death that hostility through it. So he came and proclaimed peace to you who were far off and peace to those who were near; for through him both of us have access in one Spirit to the Father".* 'Both groups' here implies the Jews and non-Jews (Gentiles) who were ever hostile to one another.

Breaking down the dividing wall, uniting hostile groups into one, and establishing peace through reconciliation were the three objectives realized through the suffering and death of Lord Jesus Christ on the cross.

Liberating oneself from the forces of sin and evil that are at work within one's own self is the first step in one's quest for true peace and happiness in life.

"If anyone makes himself clean from all those evil things, he will be used for special purposes, because he is dedicated and useful to his Master, ready to be used for every good deed," St. Paul taught his beloved disciple Timothy (2 Tim. 2:21). A truly spiritual person has to keep oneself ever pure and ready to be used by God for higher and nobler purposes. This will mean that one has to be liberated from all forces of sin and evil. This self-purification process must begin with one's own mind and body.

Controlling the senses and sensual desires is a very important requirement for self-purification. This is a challenging process wherein grace and effort have to work together. For example, a man who wants to be liberated from his slavery to the evil of alcoholism will have to be prepared to go through the 'withdrawal symptoms' which can be painful and very difficult to go through. This is where *Sahana Yoga* becomes *'mukti marga'* for him. Similarly, a patient may have to be ready to suffer the pain of injection/operation if he is to be liberated from the sickness of his body. The sleepless presence of his mother near his sickbed can liberate the little boy from his fears. For the mother, it is *Sahana Yoga*. For the child, her presence is a means of liberation from fear. This redemptive law of Christ (*Sahana Yoga Mukti Marga*) can be expanded to include a whole family, community or nation. The Gandhian movement for the political freedom of India is the best example of such collective application of *Sahana Yoga* for liberation of a whole nation. Martin Luther King Jr. and Nelson Mandela as well as many other great men and women also have applied this redemptive law in the contexts of their own social, religious and political struggles.

One individual who is willing to suffer unto death for a worthy cause can become a source of liberation for the whole community/society/nation/world. Every great human achievement has behind it a story of applied *Sahana Yoga* by one or few committed persons. In fact, nothing worthwhile can ever be achieved without paying a price for it. This price we pay for any worthwhile achievement constitutes a form of *Sahana Yoga*.

Sahana Yoga, when applied to relationships, can lead to unity and oneness (*aikya*). For example, a strained marital relationship can be healed and unity among the spouses can be re-established when they are prepared to let go of their pride and self-righteous attitudes and are ready to apologize to one another and amend their attitudes. A long-standing friendship that is broken due to a misunderstanding can be healed and renewed when both parties let go of their ego and apologize to one another. This principle can also be applied to communities, nations, and religions.

Letting go of one's ego and pride, and accepting one's own failures and mistakes and apologizing for them are acts of *Sahana Yoga* that will lead to unity and oneness. Re-establishing unity and oneness are thus the second important application of *Sahana Yoga*.

Establishing peace and harmony is the third important application of *Sahana Yoga*. *Shanti* (peace) has three important dimensions - personal, social and ecological. Peace at personal level needs forgiveness and reconciliation. We need to forgive those who have offended us. We also need to seek forgiveness from others and compensate for the damages caused by us. Restitution is an essential requirement for reconciliation.

Justice is the foundation of peace in the society. Justice has economic, social, political and religious dimensions. Our demands for justice must not lead to injustice and violence towards others.

In a society where the rich and powerful exploit the weak and helpless, collective struggles for justice will become inevitable. Many will have to suffer willingly and consciously for establishing justice and to usher in a culture of peace based on justice in the world. Environmental health and a life in harmony with nature are also essential for ecological peace.

To have the humility to seek forgiveness or to have the generosity to extend forgiveness one needs to let go of one's pride, selfishness and ego. This again is applied *Sahana Yoga*. Similarly, justice in the society may need a concerted effort by victims of injustice. Non-violent public campaigns and people's movements may become necessary. This will involve accepting willing and conscious sufferings upon themselves by many social activists committed to justice which again is *Sahana Yoga* in action for peace.

Similarly, peace with the world of nature will demand use of environment-friendly technologies and renewable energy sources, eco-friendly life-styles and food habits and an 'ethic of enough'. These can be seen as *Sahana Yoga* applied for ecological harmony and peace in the world.

Thus, we can apply *Sahana Yoga* fruitfully and make it redemptive at all levels and in all matters and places where we need liberation, unity, and peace (*mukti, aikya* and *shanti*). The results will speak for themselves.

Those who have mastered the art and science of *Sahana Yoga* will enjoy true liberation, unity and peace. They will be *jeevan muktas* (liberated persons while still alive). They will become invincible and irresistible like the Lord and Master of *Sahana Yoga*, Sadguru Jesus Christ. *Sahana Yoga* is nothing new. It has always existed at the heart of the created world as the source of creation and evolution.

As we have already seen, *Sahana Yoga* is the art and science of conscious and willing acceptance of all pains and sufferings. It is the art and science of transforming these sufferings into means of self-purification and collective spiritual growth through total self-surrender to God with faith, love and hope, following the example of Sadguru Jesus Christ. Such pains and sufferings can be the consequences of conscious and deliberate actions for liberating oneself and others from injustice, oppression and all other forces of sin and evil; for bringing about unity and harmony among people, families, religions and nations; and for establishing peace within and among individuals/families/ societies/ nations/ religions in the world.

Sahana Yoga is thus the art and science of becoming Christ-like persons by embodying the Christ-Consciousness in our own selves and putting it into practice in our own lives. It is the integral spirituality of the 'cross' that the Christian leaders are called to understand well and practice all through their lives. They will thus be able to share in the cross of Christ and be partners with him in his mission of building the Kingdom of God   (*Dharma Rajya*) of love, unity, peace and joy on the earth.

e.   Gandhian application of *Sahana Yoga*:

Preaching Christianity in India without focusing on *the* Way of Christ (*Sahana Yoga*) will be a mere waste of time. What India needs is practical applications of *Sahana Yoga* as it was taught and embodied by Sadguru Jesus Christ. Mahatma Gandhi understood this truth well and applied it for the political freedom of India.

India is the only country in the world that was able to win her political freedom by applying *Sahana Yoga* in a very dynamic and creative manner against the greatest Christian empire of the time. Gandhiji's 'Satyagraha' was a socio-spiritual application of *Sahana Yoga* for the political freedom of India from British subjugation. Hence, one can also refer to Mahatma Gandhi as an 'Indian Christ' just as the Catholic Church refers to St. Francis of Assisi as the 'second Christ'. We have developed an interreligious *sadhana* (spiritual exercise) and eco-spiritual ideology termed '*Tyagarchana*' for socio-spiritual unity and eco-spiritual regeneration of India and the world. '*Tyagarchana*' is presented as Constituent-8 of the 'Indian face of the Christian faith'.

Constituent – 7

Holistic Philosophy

The liberative Spirituality of *'Sahana Yoga'* needs to be supplemented and complemented with a holistic philosophy to realize the vision of *'Dharma Rajya'*. The philosophy developed by us over the years for this purpose is termed *'Dharmodaya'*. It is a holistic philosophy of peace with the following three constituents:

a.   Seven socio-spiritual laws of peace termed *'Satpa Rishi'*.

b.   Five principles of interreligious dialogue termed *'Pancha Tatva'*.

c.   Nine pearls of Indian wisdom termed *'Nava Ratna'*.

These three constituents of the *'Dharmodaya'* holistic philosophy are briefly explained below.

a.   *'Sapta Rishi'*

The Indian term *'Sapta Rishi'* is used to denote a constellation of seven stars. However, in the context of our mission this term is used to represent seven socio-spiritual laws of peace. These seven socio-spiritual laws of peace are developed, tested and clarified by us over the years as the basic constituent of Dharmodaya

Philosophy for the 'Indian face of the Christian faith'. The *'Sapta Rishi'* consists of:

1. The source of true and lasting love, unity, peace and happiness in the world is the grace of God that is available to all who surrender themselves willingly and consciously to Divine Providence following the example of Sadguru Jesus Christ.

2. Repentance, forgiveness, and reconciliation are pre-conditions for divine grace to take root and bear fruit in our lives.

3. All religions, scriptures and saints of humankind are recipients and reservoirs of divine grace and hence, by sincerely adhering to the eternal moral and spiritual values taught by them any one can come to a deeper experience and understanding of the grace of God.

4. The grace of God, once received, can be nurtured and nourished best by working selflessly and courageously to uphold, protect and promote truth, righteousness and peace (*satya, dharma & shanti*) in the world.

5. *'Sahana Yoga'*, the liberative spirituality of forgiving, enduring and self-sacrificing love taught and demonstrated to the world by Sadguru Jesus Christ, is the best and most effective way to promote truth, righteousness and peace in the world, and to bring about non-violent individual and social transformation.

6. Truth, righteousness and peace in the world begins with truth, righteousness and peace within individuals and families.

7. A culture of truth, righteousness and peace in the world is impossible without dialogue and cooperation among religions in the world.

These are time-tested socio-spiritual laws of peace that can be experimented with individually or collectively by anyone anywhere anytime. The results will speak for themselves.

b.   'Pancha Tatva'

There are five principles (*Pancha Tatva*) of interreligious dialogue and cooperation developed by us that will lead to harmony and cooperation among various religions for a culture of peace and sustainable development in the world. These five principles of interreligious dialogue and cooperation were first lived and taught by Sadguru Jesus Christ. Mahatma Gandhi gave them concrete practical expressions in the modern world. Hence, these principles are also termed 'Christo-Gandhian Principles'. These principles also have their roots deep in the socio-spiritual culture and traditions of India. The five Christo-Gandhian Principles constituting the *Pancha Tatva* are:

1.   Rootedness (*Sthiratha*)
2.   Openness (*Udarata*)
3.   Simplicity (*Saadagi*)
4.   Prayerfulness (*Prarthanamayata*)
5.   Non-violence (*Ahimsa*)

These five constituents of *Pancha Tatva* are briefly explained below:

1.   Rootedness (*Sthiratha*): This principle implies that we need to be rooted where we are 'planted' by God. We are planted in a family, community, nation, religion and culture by Divine Providence. We need to imbibe and make our own the best of the values and traditions of our respective families, communities, nations, religions and cultures with gratitude, respect and appreciation. We also need to strive courageously, incessantly, and prayerfully to change the values and traditions

of our families, communities, nations, religions and cultures that are not in harmony with the truth and righteousness that should help to usher in a culture of love, peace and sustainable development in the world. Ultimately, all of us have to be rooted in the one true God – the omnipotent, omniscient, and omnipresent Supreme Spirit – who is the Source of all life and Ground of all existence, and in whom we live, move, and have our being. This rootedness in God will enable us to see the truth, goodness, and beauty in all religious and cultural traditions of humankind and in the whole creation. Religious conversions and cultural alienations often go against this foundational principle of interreligious dialogue and cooperation. Hence, they are to be avoided.

2. Openness (*Udarata*): 'Openness' implies being open to the truth, goodness and beauty in all religions and scriptures, in all cultures and traditions, and in all individuals, families, communities and nations. We need to look at other religions, scriptures, cultures and traditions with respect and appreciation. Sadguru Jesus Christ was open to all. He was also appreciative of the inherent goodness and divinity of all human beings. He loved and served sinners and saints, Jews and Gentiles, Greek and Romans... all alike. Only an individual who is deeply rooted in the truth, goodness, and beauty of his/her own culture, religion and scripture can be truly open to the truth, goodness and beauty of other religions and scriptures as well as of other cultures and traditions without being insecure or being threatened by them in any manner. The more we are open to others, the more we ourselves will be enriched. Human mind, like a parachute, functions best only when it is fully open.

3. Simplicity (*Saadagi*): 'Simplicity' implies keeping our needs and wants to the optimum. Aircrafts and motor vehicles have optimum speeds at which the fuel consumption is the least. The fuel consumption increases if the speed is below or above the optimum. This principle applies to human beings and their communities too. Consumption has to be kept to an optimum level so that the health of one's body, soul, family, society and nation, as well as of the Earth Family as a whole, is maintained at its best.

4. Prayerfulness (*Prarthanamayata*): 'Prayerfulness' implies being open to the living presence of God in one's own life, in others' lives and in the whole creation. Sadguru Jesus Christ was a deeply prayerful person. He often withdrew to lonely places to pray, and be alone with the Alone, the Source and Ground of his being. As a result, he could experience the oneness of reality, and his own intimate communion with God. His life was a living prayer of joy and gratitude. Prayerfulness is also an antidote for the dangers of consumerism and materialism. It is not saying many prayers. It is an expression of one's gratitude for the gift of life. It is living from the depth of one's being. Prayer establishes a conscious connectivity with God, in whom we live, move, and have our being. 'Prayer' can mean different things for different people depending upon the levels of their spiritual growth. It also varies from religion to religion. But the ultimate goal of all prayers is to establish an abiding connectivity with God, the Source and Ground of existence, in whom we live, move, and have our being.

5. Non-violence (*Ahimsa*): According to Mahatma Gandhi 'non-violence' is love in action. It comes from a harmonious and prayerful life. Lord Jesus Christ taught his disciples to love their enemies and pray for those who persecuted them. Rising

above the agony of his own sufferings and death on the cross, he prayed for those who crucified him. This he did because of his deep love for them. *Ahimsa Paramo Dharma* (Non-violence is the supreme virtue) is a dictum representing India's deep faith in non-violence. Truth and non-violence (*satya* and *ahimsa*) were the two constituents of the spiritual weapon of *Satyagraha* that Mahatma Gandhi had developed to fight the outside 'enemy' non-violently. St. Francis of Assisi was an embodiment of non-violence. The wild and ferocious wolf was also a 'brother' to him. He was in total harmony with all living beings and with the whole Nature.

A culture of abiding peace can emerge on earth only when we are awakened to the interdependence and interrelatedness of all human beings and all other living beings. By harming others, we also harm ourselves. By destroying Nature, we are destroying ourselves. Non-violence is harmonious coexistence. It is an important virtue promoted by different enlightened religious traditions of humankind. Violence begets more violence. Stockpiling more weapons of mutual destruction cannot bring peace to the world. In fact, the nations with more weapons in their arsenals tend to be more violent.

These five principles of interreligious harmony and cooperation are also time-tested principles which anyone can apply and see the results for himself/herself.

c.   'Navaratna'

The word *nava* means nine. *Ratna* means pearls. 'Nava Ratna' implies nine pearls of Indian wisdom drawn from India's own spiritual and cultural treasures.

The nine constituent elements of the *Nava Ratna* are:

1. *'Prajnanam Brahma'*
2. *'Ekam Sat Vipra Bahudha Vadanti'*
3. *'Ishavasyamidam Sarvam'*
4. *'Vasudhaiva Kutumbakam'*
5. *'Sarva Dharma Sadbhav'*
6. *'Satyameva Jayate'*
7. *'Ahimsa Paramodharma'*
8. *'Purushartha'*
9. *'Chaturashrama'*

The nine constituents of *Nava Ratna* are briefly explained below.

1. *'Prajnanam Brahma'*: This implies that *Brahma* (God), the Source of all being and Ground of all existence, is *Prajna* (Consciousness). We live, move, and have our being in this Universal Consciousness. Everything is created through, with, and from this Universal Consciousness. Everything exists *in* this Universal Consciousness and *because of* this Universal Consciousness. This is the deepest insight into the nature of the Ultimate Reality experienced and taught by the enlightened saints and sages of ancient India. This Universal Consciousness is also the 'Word of God', the Christ Consciousness that was with God and that was God, and through whom all things are created (Jn. 1:1-5). The Word of God incarnated in human history as Jesus of Nazareth through whom grace and truth came to humankind (Jn. 1:14-17). This insight is the spiritual foundation of the *Dharmodaya* holistic philosophy.

2. *'Ekam Sat Vipra Bahudha Vadanti'*: This implies that the Ultimate Truth, God, is one, but the saints/wise men in the world refer to this Ultimate Truth by various names. However, this one true God is beyond all names, forms and attributes ever comprehended and ever comprehensible by human intellect.

Yet, the human person can develop an intimate personal relationship with this one true God, following the example of Sadguru Jesus Christ. Hence, it is foolish to fight or argue in the name of God and religion. The Self-revelations of God within individuals and in this world are bound with time and space, and are determined by the context and the level of consciousness of the person/ community/ religion concerned.

3. *'Isa Vasyam Idam Sarvam'*: This implies that God pervades the whole creation. We live, move, and have our being in God (Acts 17: 28). Creation is the Self-expression of God bound with time and space. Hence, the whole creation is sacred. Every human person, every living being, and Mother Earth as a whole, need to be treated with gentleness, respect and caring love. Everyone and everything are unique and important in the creative plan of God. The human spirit is created in the image and likeness of the Divine Spirit. Hence, it is holy and eternally divine. All discriminations in the name of religion, nationality, party, language, ethnicity, gender, caste, class, colour, creed etc. are crimes against God and humanity. Damages to ecological harmony and environmental health are also crimes against God and fellow living beings.

4. *'Vasudhaiva Kutumbakam'*: This implies that all living beings inhabiting our planet Earth together constitute one large Earth Family bound with a common destiny. The COVID-19 pandemic has taught us this truth in a very painful manner so that we might never forget it. The varieties of trees, plants and creepers; all species of animals, fishes, birds, reptiles; and the humankind together form this Earth Family. The human species constitute the most advanced species among all living beings on earth. Human beings are called to be like 'elder brothers and sisters' to all other living beings. Hence, we need

to take loving care of all living beings inhabiting our planet which is our 'Common Home' in the Solar System.

5. *'Sarva Dharma Sadbhav'*: This means that we need to give equal respect to all religions and their Scriptures. Religions are collective expressions of humanity's eternal quest for Truth and for the meaning and purpose of life in this world and thereafter. There exists a great deal of truth, goodness and beauty in every religious tradition. Hence, religions can help very much in humanity's moral and spiritual development and in promoting peace and happiness on earth if understood and applied in the right manner. No religion can claim the monopoly of truth, God or salvation.

6. *'Satyameva Jayate'*: This means that truth alone will succeed in the end. Adherence to truth is a prerequisite for developing integrity of character and for unity of vision and mission that are essential for a meaningful and fruitful life. Mahatma Gandhi proclaimed from his own experience: 'Truth is God'. Adherence to truth was an integral part of his quest for God. *'Satyameva Jayate'* is also the National Motto of India.

7. *'Ahimsa Paramo Dharma'*: This means that 'non-violence is the highest virtue'. Violence begets more violence. 'An eye for an eye will only make the whole world blind' pointed out Mahatma Gandhi who was a great apostle of peace and non-violence. His birthday, 02 October, is declared as *International Day of Non-violence* by the United Nations.

8. *'Purushartha'*: The term *'Purushartha'* is a Sanskrit word that can be translated as the 'objects of human pursuit' or 'goals of man.' It is a derivation of the Sanskrit word *purusha,* meaning 'person,' and *artha* meaning 'purpose.' The *Prushartha* presented and promoted by the enlightened saints and sages of India

consists of four important goals of human life in this world which according to them are right values (*Dharma*), earning wealth in the right manner (*Artha*), enjoying the pleasures of life in the right way (*Kama*), and attaining heaven (*Moksha*). Generating wealth and enjoying the legitimate pleasures of life in the right way are essential for a healthy, happy and peaceful life in this world.

In its true spiritual sense, the Indian concept of '*tyaga*' (renunciation) does not mean rejection of wealth and pleasures. It means a rejection of slavery or attachment to them. We should not allow wealth and pleasures to conquer our minds. The mind should always be able to control them. Breathing and eating are essential for life, but breathing and eating cannot be the goals of life. Wealth and pleasures are essential for happy life. But they should never be the goals of life. Transcendence, not rejection, is the way of spiritual growth and abiding peace.

9. '*Chaturashrama*': The term *Chaturashrama* means four *Ashramas* or stages of life. The *Chaturashrama* constitutes a holistic vision of life in which human life in this world is divided into four stages. It is also yet another great contribution of India to the social development and well-being of the human race.

The first of the four stages are *Brahamcharya* (stage of celibate studentship). This is until about 25 years of age. Then comes *Grahastha* (the stage of married family life). This is from 25 years till about 50 years of age. After completing the family responsibilities by 50 years or so, one is expected to enter *Vanaprastha* (stage of contemplative life in the forest). This would last till about 75 years of age. Then one enters the fourth and final stage which is the stage of *Sanyasa*. This is a stage of total self-surrender and renunciation as a preparation for the final journey from this world to the Beyond.

We have slightly modified this ancient version of *Chaturashrama* in order to make it more relevant to our modern era. The third *Ashrama* in the ancient Indian tradition was *'Vanaprastha'*. This is modified in the context of the present era as *Seva Ashrama* (stage of selfless service to society for fulfilling one's social responsibilities). This will be from 50 to 65 years of age. The *Sanyasa Ashrama* will be from 65 to 75 years of age. This is the stage of renunciation of all physical and emotional relationships and attachments. After the *Sanyasa Ashrama*, we have added yet another stage termed *'Ativarna Ashrama'* which is the final stage of integration and witness wherein one achieves a final integration in one's life and mission, and becomes a living witness to the love, peace, freedom and joy of an abiding communion with the one true God, the omnipotent, omnipresent and omniscient Supreme Spirit.

Through the *Seva Ashrama,* the third stage of life becomes more relevant to the contemporary world. The society we live in, has been contributing in many ways towards helping us to become what we are today. Hence, we have a responsibility towards the society. This responsibility is to be fulfilled before we enter the *Sanyasa Ashrama.*

The *Sanyasa* stage of total renunciation too is to be transcended to a higher stage of integration. Renunciation by itself can also be seen as a stage in our quest for a higher form of integration in life. Hypothesis, Thesis, Antithesis and Synthesis are often the four stages followed in scientific research for acquiring scientific knowledge and for achieving scientific progress and development. These four stages of scientific research can also be applied effectively in our spiritual quest/life.

The above nine 'Sanatana Dharma insights' are truly Indian and truly universal. These are together termed *'Nava Ratna'* because they constitute the nine 'pearls' of India's ancient wisdom.

The *Sapta Rishi, Pancha Tatva* and *Nava Ratna* presented above, together constitute the *'Dharmodaya'* holistic philosophy. This is a philosophy of love, peace, and sustainable development.

If *Dharmodaya* is put into practice sincerely, we will be able to establish the unity of all life and the solidarity of whole humankind. 'We, the Children of Eternity' (*Amritasya Putra*) will then be able to transform the pandemic-devastated world into the *'Dharma Rajya'* (kingdom of God) of love, righteousness, peace and reconciliation.

Dharmodaya will also enable us to understand the interdependent organic nature of planet Earth. Practical applications of the holistic philosophy of *Dharmodaya* will help us to spiritualize economics and politics, and rebuild science and technology on a new and strong foundation of love. Economics and politics are two dimensions of our collective existence that affect the lives of all people. These are interdependent and interrelated like the two sides of a coin. All economic decisions in the world today are political decisions, and all political decisions are influenced by economic considerations. A spiritualization of economics and politics is the crying need of the modern era enslaved by the competitive consumerism and self-destructive materialism.

Spiritualizing politics and economics and rebuilding science and technology on a new foundation of love will constitute the two very challenging tasks ahead of the world in the third millennium. India has an important role to play in this twofold challenging task.

Christian leaders and the Christian Churches in India are called to help the nation in this challenging mission of the third millennium by giving practical expressions to the holistic philosophy of *Dharmodaya* inspired by the vision of *Dharma Rajya* and empowered by the liberative spirituality of *Sahana Yoga*.

Constituent – 8

Eco-Spiritual Ideology

A 'philosophy' presents an overall vision of life and reality. It encompasses all dimensions and stages of life. Whereas an 'ideology' is system-specific. It is also bound with time and space. An ideology constitutes the 'cutting edge' of a philosophy.

A vision needs a philosophy to sustain it, but it needs an ideology to realize it. A vision without an ideology to realize it and an ideology without a vision ahead of it will not bear fruit. The existing materialistic and consumerist ideologies like Capitalism, Communism, Socialism etc. have outlived their utility and will not be able to help us build a world of peace and sustainable development. They are based on a materialistic philosophy and a consumerist culture. They lack the integral vision of life and reality and the eco-spiritual worldview without which abiding peace and sustainable development in the world are impossible. History bears testimony to this truth. The present era calls for an eco-spiritual ideology that can spiritualize economics and politics, and rebuild science and technology on a new foundation of love.

An eco-spiritual ideology termed *'Tyagarchana'* is developed by us to provide a strong ideological foundation for the vision of an Integrated World Order.

'*Tyagarchana*' was originally developed by us as an interreligious *sadhana* for spiritual unity and purification of India. It is further developed over the years as an eco-spiritual ideology for a culture of love, peace and sustainable development in the world.

The term '*Tyagarchana*' is comprised of two words '*tyaga*' and '*archana*'. '*Tyaga*' means renunciation or sacrifice. It is used here to mean voluntary sacrifice of something that is dear to one's heart. '*Archana*' means an offering made to God with love. Selfless service rendered to the poor and needy fellow human beings with love is the best form of '*Archana*' that we can offer to God. We can see God in and through the creation, especially in and through other human beings. Hence, serving others with love is serving God with love. "Just as you did it to one of the least of these, you did it to me" proclaimed Sadguru Jesus Christ (Mt 25: 40).

a.   Definition & Forms of *Tyagarchana*

'*Tyagarchana*' can be defined as '*Voluntary sacrifice of something dear to one's heart and using the time, energy, and/or money saved from such voluntary sacrifices for rendering selfless service to the needy fellow human beings with love.*' It has three constituents; love, sacrifice and service.

There can be very many forms and examples of *Tyagarchana*. Skipping a meal and using the saving to feed a hungry person with love is an act of *Tyagarchana*. Giving up the coffee, tea or alcoholic drinks that one likes and using the savings to pay hospital bills of a poor person with love is also an inspiring example of *Tyagarchana*. Giving up celebrations of birthdays, wedding anniversaries, feasts, festivals etc. and using the savings to educate poor children with love; giving up the pursuits of selfish ambitions and pleasures and finding time to be with one's own family and children; taking care of one's old parents or sick neighbors with love at the cost of one's own comfort; giving one's reserved seat in the bus/train with love to an old/sick person without reservation; giving up ice creams/ chocolates/ sweets and other luxury items and using the amounts thus saved for feeding/educating poor children with love; accepting upon oneself the sufferings and pains for promoting social justice; participating in non-violent public campaigns and going to jail for a worthy cause; fasting and praying for the good of others or for social transformation and systemic change; making some sacrifice and contributing the amount/time thus saved for supporting voluntary groups/ citizens' initiatives/ social and religious organizations/ people's movements for common good with love, are examples of various acts of *Tyagarchana*.

Willing acceptance of all sufferings and pains in one's life and offering them to God with love for the purification and spiritual development of oneself and others is *Tyagarchana* of a greater spiritual quality.

Tyagarchana can have very many redemptive expressions and applications in our day to day lives to fight the inner enemies of selfishness, pride, greed, lust, anger etc.

'God is love' is the truth experienced and taught by the enlightened saints and sages of humankind. It is by serving the needy fellow human beings with love that we can serve God. '*Manav Seva Madhav Seva*' (service to humanity is service to God) is an Indian dictum representing this truth.

Willing sacrifice and loving service (*Tyaga* and *seva*) are the two constituents of *Tyagarchana. Tyaga* and *seva* are like the two sides of the coin of *Tyagarchana.* These are the eternal values that have ever inspired the Indian mind.

"Renunciation and service are the eternal ideals that have ever

inspired the Indian mind. Strengthen her in those channels and the rest will take care of itself" was the conviction of Swami Vivekananda, the great patriot-saint of India.

"Love God with all your heart, all your mind, all your soul and all your strength; and love your neighbor as you love yourself" & *"First you seek the Kingdom of God and His righteousness. Everything else will also be added unto you,"* taught Sadguru Jesus Christ. *"I have come that they may have life, and that they may have it more abundantly"* & *"Peace I leave with you. My peace I give to you; not as the world gives do I give to you. Let not your heart be troubled, neither let it be afraid."* He had also assured and encouraged his disciples.

"No country has ever risen without being purified through the fire of suffering. Mother suffers so that her child may live. The condition for wheat-growing is that the seed grain should perish. Life comes out of death. Will India rise out of her slavery without fulfilling this eternal law of purification through suffering? Progress is to be measured by the amount of suffering undergone by the sufferer. The purer the suffering, the greater the progress," were the words of wisdom and experience of Mahatma Gandhi.

As seen above, *Tyagarchana* involves sacrificing something we like voluntarily and using the time, energy, or money saved from such voluntary sacrifices to serve the needy fellow human beings with love. It is the *sadhana* (spiritual exercise) of love, righteousness, peace and reconciliation. It is also a *sadhana* shared by different religious traditions in the world for liberation, unity and peace.

Above all, *Tyagarchna* will help us to counter the onslaughts of the spiritless & lifeless materialism, and selfish & violent consumerism that are spreading all over the world today and are threatening the very existence of the human race on earth.

b.   Kinds of *Tyagarchana*

Tyagarchana can be broadly divided into four kinds:

- *Tyagarchana* of time

- *Tyagarchana* of professional service

- *Tyagarchana* of energy

- *Tyagarchana* of money

Tyagarchana of time implies giving up something one likes and using the time thus saved to be with needy fellow human beings with love. Giving up watching one's favourite TV serial/ entertainment programme/ cinema and using that time to be with other needy fellow human beings with love are examples of *Tyagarchana* of time.

Tyagarchana of professional service implies acts of extending selfless professional help to the needy with love. Teaching, healthcare, extending intellectual/technical service to the needy etc. are examples of *Tyagarchana* of professional service.

Working with one's own hands to support /help others, offering one's reserved seat in the bus/train to an old/sick person; extending physical help to the needy etc. are examples of *Tyagarchana* of energy.

Tyagarchana of money implies sacrificing something we like and using the money saved from such sacrifices to help the needy with love. Skipping a meal, fasting for a day, giving up birthday/ wedding anniversary celebrations, giving up luxury items, walking or cycling to one's work place nearby instead of using motor vehicles etc. and using the money thus saved to help the needy with love are examples of *Tyagarchana* of money.

c.   Eco-spiritual ideology of *Tyagarchana*

Tyagarchana is essentially an interreligious *sadhana* of liberation, purification, unity, and peace. When it is put into large scale application in economic, political, social, religious or ecological dimensions of life, it becomes a holistic eco-spiritual ideology.

An economic system under the *Tyagarchana* ideology will have to promote Cooperative/Partnership/Trusteeship enterprises in place of Public/Private/Monopoly enterprises. All of us are members of one human family bound with a common destiny. This truth is reaffirmed beyond all doubts by the COVID-19 pandemic. 'Master & Slave'/ 'Owner & Worker'/ 'Capitalist & Labour'/ 'Employee & Employer' etc. are terminologies and relationships that are opposed to this truth of the unity and solidarity of humankind.

The *Tyagarchana* eco-spiritual ideology demands and will lead to a moral and spiritual regeneration of our economic, political, social, religious and ecological systems and institutions. Moral and spiritual regeneration implies first of all a decentralization of these systems and institutions in order to make them more transparent, accountable, people-centered & environment-friendly based on the concepts of Unitive Eco-Spiritual Consciousness & Collective Eco-Spiritual Responsibility. This is an essential prerequisite for giving practical expressions to the *Tyagarchana* eco-spiritual ideology in the economic, social, political, religious and ecological dimensions of our collective life.

Tyagarchana is both an interreligious sadhana as well as a socio-spiritual ideology of love, sacrifice and service. It can be applied at individual/family/community/national/global level depending on the need and context of application. This is the uniqueness of the eco-spiritual ideology of *Tyagarchana*.

Tyagarchana can be applied at all levels; from the individual level to the global level. No other ideology has such flexibility and universality. '*Tyagarchana*' will remain forever a great and unique contribution of India to human thought and development.

d.   *Sanatana Dharma* **pillars of** *Tyagarchana*

The following four pearls of wisdom from the '*Navaratna*' of '*Dharmodaya*' holistic philosophy are adopted as the four '*Sanatana Dharma*' pillars of *Tyagarchana*:

1. '*Prajnanam Brahma*' (Aitareya Upanishad): *Brahma* (God), the Source of all being and Ground of all existence, is *Prajna* (Consciousness). We live, move, and have our being in this Universal Consciousness. Everything is created through, with, and from this Universal Consciousness.

2. '*Ekam Sat Vipra Bahudha Vadanti*' (Rig Veda): The Ultimate Truth is one, but the saints/ the wise people in the world refer to it by various names.

3. '*Isa Vasyam Idam Sarvam*' (Ishavasya Upanishad): God pervades the whole creation. Creation is the Self-expression of God bound with time and space.

4. '*Vasudhaiva Kutumbakam*' (Maha Upanishad): All living beings inhabiting our planet Earth together constitute one large Earth Family bound with a common destiny. The COVID-19 pandemic has taught us this truth in a very painful manner so that we might never forget it.

The above four Sanatana Dharma insights are truly Indian and truly universal at the same time. These are together termed '*Sanatana Dharma Chatushtayam*' of *Tyagarchana*. The socio-spiritual ideology of '*Tyagarchana*' built on the foundations of *Sanatana Dharma Chatushtayam* will help us to spiritualize economics and politics, and rebuild science and technology on a new foundation of love.

(NB: Please refer to previous chapter above for explanations of these four 'Sanatana Dharma' pillars of *Tyagarchana*).

e.   Value-addition through *Tyagarchana*

An amount of money can have a spiritual value added to it, in addition to its monetary value, when it is saved through loving sacrifices. This spiritual value has the power to transform us and others and bring out the best in all of us. The ability to add spiritual values to time, money and service is within the reach of every human person.

Tyagarchana helps to purify ourselves and develop in us an attitude of gratitude. It will motivate us to accept all pains and sufferings in our lives willingly and consciously and offer them to God with love for the redemptive purification and spiritual growth of ourselves and others. It is an interreligious and a socio-spiritual ideology for reducing the selfishness, pride, greed, lust and anger lurking in our hearts. It will bring showers of divine blessings upon us and others when we sincerely practice it. It will also help us find abiding peace and happiness within.

The eco-spiritual ideology of *Tyagarchana* and the divine grace received through it can liberate us from the forces of evil, and from the grip of *Karma* (for Hindus), *Kismet* (for Muslims), *Destiny* (for Christians), which often implies a law by which we are helplessly bound to our previous actions.

Tyagarchana, when accepted and practiced by a group of people, can generate a greater amount of synergy (collective spiritual energy) which can be channelized creatively for higher goals and nobler purposes.

'Unless a grain of wheat falls into the ground and dies, it remains single. But when it dies, it grows into a new plant that will produce grains a hundred fold' taught Sadguru Jesus Christ. No nation can ever become great without voluntarily accepting all sufferings on themselves by its citizens for the good of the nation, taught Mahatma Gandhi. We need to die to our own little 'selves' in order to bear abundant fruits for the greater good of humanity and for the glory of God.

The socio-spiritual ideology of *Tyagarchana* has hidden within it great spiritual energy that can liberate individuals/communities/nations/religions from the various forces of evil/injustice/superstition/exploitation/oppression. Mahatma Gandhi had understood this truth well. He had developed 'Satyagraha' as a spiritual weapon based on this truth to liberate India from unjust British subjugation and exploitation.

f.   Fighting the inner enemies through *Tyagarchana*

The 'enemy' today is not an outside force. Our enemies now are within and among us. Selfishness, greed, pride, lust, anger etc. are the enemies that we need to fight today. These evil forces which are active within and among us have been the real causes for most of human sufferings in the world. These enemies cannot be fought and overcome with the socio-political weapon of Satyagraha. This realization had prompted us to undertake studies and experiments for developing the eco-spiritual ideology of *Tyagarchana* to fight and overcome the 'enemies' which are active within and among us today.

The Christian mystics say that the 'cross' (self-sacrificing love) is at the heart of history. It is also at the source and center of the created world. Creation advances in its evolutionary growth through the path of cross. 'Nations like individuals can be redeemed only with the power of the cross,' was the conviction of Mahatma Gandhi. This realization was the inspiration for him to develop

'*Satyagraha*'. Suffering, when accepted willingly and consciously for a higher goal or purpose, can generate great amount of synergy and liberative power.

Lord Jesus Christ went through the agony of suffering and death on the cross for no fault of his. He was crucified by selfish, greedy, proud, ignorant, arrogant and prejudiced religious leaders. Those of us who have these forces of evil present in our own lives are also 'partners' in crucifying Christ because humanity is a socio-spiritual continuum beyond time-space limitations. We are all united to one another in the continuous flow of human history and in the evolutionary process of human consciousness.

Even while dying on the cross, rising above the agony of excruciating pain, the Divine Master prayed for those who crucified him. Through his death and prayer on the cross he 'redeemed' those who crucified him from their sins.   All those who accept him as the Lord and Master of their lives and surrender their sufferings to God as part of the cross of their Divine Master can also share this redemptive mission of Christ on the cross. This is the 'mystery' of the cross. It is in this 'mystery of the cross' that human suffering can find its true meaning and purpose, and its great potentials and possibilities.

It is by willing and conscious acceptance of suffering for higher goals and purposes and surrendering them to God as part of the cross of Christ that disciples of Sadguru Jesus Christ can become partners with their Divine Master in the redemption of the human race. This principle is applied effectively through the eco-spiritual ideology of *Tyagarchana*.

The eco-spiritual ideology of *Tyagarchana* will not only help us to transform India but will also empower India to help transform the post-pandemic world into the *Vasudhaiva Kutumbakam* (Earth

Family) as envisioned by her enlightened saints and sages from time immemorial.

(NB: for further details of the ideology of *Tyagarchana*, please refer chapter-4b of the book 'Integral Renaissance of India'/ chapter-7 of the book 'A New Creation in Christ' / chapter-3B of the mission manual of Tyagarchana Shanti Mission.)

Constituent – 9

Enlightened Christian Leadership

'Enlightened Christian leadership' implies leadership guided by the indwelling light of Christ. It is leadership with the wisdom and power of God in Christ. Such enlightened Christian leadership is a very essential requirement for rebuilding the pandemic-devastated and violence-ridden world on a peace and sustainable development paradigm.

The following five foundational principles, five core values and five personal attributes of enlightened leadership are developed and adopted by us for the Enlightened Christian Leadership.

a.   Five Foundation Principles

The five foundational principles of enlightened Christian leadership are:

1.   'Focus & Progress'

The first principle of enlightened Christian leadership is 'Focus & Progress'. Only by focusing on what one is doing, can one really make any true progress.

Fast flying fighter planes of the Air Force have very pointed cone nose and delta wings, making them look like arrows piercing through the sky at incredible speed. The smaller and more pointed an air craft is, the faster it can fly. This principle holds good for us also. With more focused thought and action we can rise higher and faster in life. We can also do better in our selected field of activity, whatever it may be. Also, we need to keep our 'core team' of decision-makers to the minimum and should remain focused on our 'core competency'. All of us can experiment with this principle and experience the results for ourselves.

In Military Academies across the world they teach 'Principles of War'. The first Principle of War is: 'selection and maintenance of an aim'. Similarly, one needs to select and maintain a goal for one's life. This goal and purpose of life should not be lost. It should be always kept in mind.

The goal of a disciple of Sadguru Jesus Christ should be to become a Christ-like person and to work for the Kingdom of God on earth with the power and wisdom of God given to him/her in, with and through the Divine Master.

2.   'Trust & Entrust'

The second principle of enlightened Christian leadership is 'Trust & Entrust'. 'Believe in God, believe also in me', told the Divine Master to his disciples (Jn 14: 1). One needs to have absolute faith in God and in Sadguru Jesus Christ. One also needs to trust oneself and others. Only those who can trust themselves alone can trust others. Without trusting people, we cannot entrust any authority and responsibility to them. Without delegation of authority and responsibility, we cannot achieve anything great in life. All great missions will need great team work which is only possible by entrusting authority and responsibility to others. This means believing in oneself first.

According to Swami Vivekananda, 'he is an atheist who does not believe in himself'. He had also pointed out: "*The old religion said that he was an atheist who did not believe in God. The new religion says that he is an atheist who does not believe in himself.*" We need to have faith in ourselves and our abilities. Only then we can have faith in others. Such faith is developed through a living and loving communion with the Christ-Spirit. Only when we entrust responsibilities to others, showing our faith in them and their capacity, will others be able to rise above themselves and shine forth in their work and mission.

3. 'Grow & Help grow'

The third principle of enlightened Christian leadership is a corollary to the second. It is: 'Grow & Help grow'. Anything challenging and worthwhile should always help us grow. Only a great and challenging vision can help to bring out the best in us. As we grow, we need to help all those working with us also to grow.

Lord Jesus Christ has given us the most challenging vision and mission that can bring out the best in us and help us become Christ-like persons. 'Seek first the Kingdom of God and His righteousness. All other things will also be given to you', assured the Divine Master to his disciples (Mt 6:33).

Seeking the Kingdom of God and His righteousness is the greatest mission anyone can undertake in this world. It is a mission that will enable everyone involved in it to grow to ever greater heights of holiness and achievement.

By helping others to grow, we ourselves will rise to greater heights. People are remembered not for what good they did for themselves, but for what good they did for others. Selfishness prevents our inner growth. Selfless service inspired by love alone can help our spiritual development. 'Unless a grain of wheat falls and dies it remains single. But when it falls into the soil and dies, it will grow as a plant and bear much fruit, sixty fold and hundred fold', taught the Divine Master (Ref. Jn 12: 24).

Activities and initiatives that cannot help us and others to grow are mere waste of precious resources, time, and energy. Time is the most precious gift of God to us. One's life-span in this world is measured in terms of time, that is, in terms of years, months, days and hours. Endeavor and achievement are our grateful response to the gift of life, to the gift of time.

'The Son of Man came to serve, not to be served', told Lord Jesus Christ, the most enlightened leader in human history, to his disciples about himself (Mt 20: 28). 'You are the light of the world' (Mt 5: 14), he reminded them. 'The leaders among you should be the servants of all', he taught them (Mk 10: 43). He was always supporting, encouraging and guiding them lovingly in their life and mission. We should also do likewise.

4.   'Risk & Rise'

The fourth principle of enlightened Christian leadership is 'Risk & Rise'. An aircraft or a kite can rise only with air resistance. Life becomes more fruitful by facing the trials and tribulations of this world with courage and faith. Without challenges, one cannot rise high in life. One also needs to take 'calculated risks' from time to time, if one has to rise to greater heights of excellence and achievement.

'Don't be afraid', Sadguru Jesus Christ kept telling his disciples. Fear is the biggest block in the path of true peace and happiness, and also in the path of success and achievements. With the coming of the Holy Spirit, the scared disciples became fearless witnesses to the power and wisdom of God revealed in, with, and through their Divine Master.

The real caliber and character of an individual is to be seen at times of adversity. Opportunities to suffer for a noble cause are also opportunities for self-purification and personal growth. Just as gold and silver are purified in fire, we, the humans are purified and sanctified through voluntary suffering for a higher cause.

Only by taking calculated risks can we really rise in life in our forward, upward, and Godward journey.

5.   'Respond & Report'

The fifth principle of enlightened Christian leadership is 'Respond & Report'. One needs to respond creatively and courageously to the demands of the time and to the challenges of life. Such creative and courageous responses are essential for making life exciting and worth living. Most of us only 'react', we do not 'respond' creatively to situations and crises. An effective response to a crisis can come only from 'creative fidelity', not from 'repetitive loyalty'.

In an organizational setup or in a group activity, we also need to 'report' to the concerned authorities who are responsible for decision-making and for the effective management of the institution, organization or group. This is very important for organizations and institutions with a well-defined hierarchy of leadership. The leader can take proper decisions and provide effective leadership only when the cadres report to him/her regularly on their work and activities, and on their achievements and failures.

Similarly, networking and linking up with various like-minded organizations, institutions, individuals and groups are very essential for creating the 'synergy' necessary for the success of our endeavors.

Effective use of communication skills is also very important for the successful implementation of the principle of 'Respond and Report'.

b.   The Five Core Values

'Love the Lord your God with all your heart, all your mind, all your soul and all your strength, and love your neighbour as you love yourself', was the eternal principle of the 'Kingdom of God' ('Dharma Rajya') initiated by Sadguru Jesus Christ in the world. Truth and Non-violence (Satya and Ahimsa) were the two core values promoted by Mahatma Gandhi, the greatest 'Apostle of Peace' in the modern world. Renunciation and Selfless Service (Tyaga and Seva) were the eternal values of India identified and promoted by Swami Vivekananda, the great Hindu patriot-saint of India. These five values (Love, Truth, Non-violence, Renunciation and Selfless Service) together constitute the 'core values' of enlightened Christian leadership.

c.   The Five Personal Attributes

The five important personal attributes of an enlightened Christian leader are Strength of Character, Courage of Conviction, Creativity, Transparency & Accountability.

An enlightened Christian leader has to be a person with strength of character and courage of conviction. He/She should have a very creative mind. He/She should be transparent in all dealings and relationships. Accountability for actions taken and words spoken and for all incomes and expenses are essential attributes of an enlightened Christian leader. He/She should also accept the full responsibility for the consequences of his/her actions and words.

These five foundational principles, five core values and five personal attributes of enlightened Christian leadership are universal in their appeal and application. They can also be effectively applied in all areas of human life and endeavor.

Constituent – 10

Christian Mission Methodologies

I realized early in my pilgrimage of faith as a disciple of Sadguru Jesus in the multi-religious context of India the need for appropriate mission methodologies, if one is to succeed in achieving the goal of one's mission.

My focus was in developing Christian Mission Methodologies that could be effectively applied to make the mission of my 'second life' bear abundant fruits for the glory of God and good of humanity. The fruits of this quest are presented below.

a.   Common Basic Mission Methodology

The Basic Mission Methodology developed and adopted by us is *'Begin with self, begin today, & begin small'*. This methodology is also being accepted and appreciated by many others today. Hence, it is also presented and promoted by us as 'Common Basic Mission Methodology'.

Peace and happiness in the world begins with peace and happiness within individuals and families. Any good work or mission must not be delayed; it must begin today itself with whatever resources that we may have. We have realized that this basic mission methodology is the best suited methodology in any socio-spiritual mission.

'Yesterday is like a cancelled cheque. Tomorrow is like a promissory note. But today is like ready cash in hand', says an old wise dictum. There is no use of wasting time by regretting about our past mistakes or by worrying about the future problems. What is past is gone forever. Time lost cannot be regained at any cost.

'Today' is the most valuable gift of God. We should make the best use of it for the glory of His name and for the good of humanity.

Life is the most precious gift of God. It is measured in terms of time. Hence, wasting time means wasting life. Time is used best when it is used for serving our needy fellow human beings. 'It is in giving that we receive' is the spiritual wisdom taught to us by saints and sages of all religions.

We cannot expect others to do what we ourselves are not prepared to do. We have no right to find fault with others when we ourselves make such mistakes. We have no moral right to criticize anyone or anything unless we have an alternative to offer. As Mahatma Gandhi had said, we should first become the change that we wish to see in the world.

Without a self-transformation, all efforts to change others and the world will be mere waste of time and energy. Self-transformation and social transformation should go hand in hand. One without the other will not last long.

It is said by the wise that a bald-headed man will not be a successful salesman of 'Kesha Vardhani oil'. ('Kesha Vardhani oil' is oil that is claimed to have the medicinal powers to make human hair grow black and thick).

Every disciple of Christ is called to be the 'light of the world' (Mt 5:14). Our light must shine before others so that they can see the good works that we are doing and praise God for the gift that we are to them and to the world. We must begin this mission today itself with purity of intentions and means, and with whatever little resources that we may have.

Having done our best, we need to trust in Divine Providence to provide the rest of the required resources and make our efforts bear abundant fruits for the glory of God and good of the world. This will need a great deal of patience and perseverance. The best things in life are got at the cost of great pain.

This Common Basic Mission Methodology is perhaps the best possible methodology for making any socio-spiritual mission bear abundant fruits. It is a methodology in which human endeavour and divine grace work together.

b.   The Professional Project Methodology (8-S Methodology)

This is an eight-stage methodology that can be used fruitfully for important projects and activities. Hence, this is also termed '8-S Methodology'.

This '8-S Methodology' consists of:

1. *Visualization*: At this first stage one is called to imagine/ visualize in one's own mind the entire project. From imagination comes creativity. Imagination is an important and essential mental activity required for the success of any major human initiative/project.

2. *Formulation*: At this second stage one is called to put down the whole proposed project in writing. This Project Plan is to be circulated among a small group of qualified

and trusted friends and co-workers for their valuable suggestions. A finalized document is to be prepared and accepted at the end of this process.

3. *Mobilization*: At this third stage one is called to mobilize the necessary human, financial, and material resources for the successful implementation of the project.

4. *Organization*: At this fourth stage one is called to set up an office, appoint necessary staff, and motivate and organize oneself and others for the successful implementation of the project.

5. *Coordination*: At this fifth stage one is called to coordinate with the staff and other individuals and agencies to get everything going smoothly for the successful implementation of the project.

6. *Implementation*: At this stage one is called to work towards achieving the objectives of the project in a time-bound and target-oriented manner. One needs to set targets and time frames for a stage-by-stage implementation of the project.

7. *Evaluation*: This seventh stage is a stage of audit and evaluation. At this stage one is called to audit the accounts and evaluate the results of the project. Tasks done, targets realized, money spent, mission completed and results achieved are to be critically evaluated at this stage.

8. *Documentation*: This is the eighth and final stage. At this stage a written report with photographs, audited accounts and other relevant documents are to be prepared and filed on the completed project. These will be helpful records and documents for future reference and study.

This Professional Project Methodology (8-S Methodology) is found to be well-accepted and very useful for the successful implementation of any important socio-spiritual project.

c.   The Growth Orientation Methodology (3-Q Methodology)

This is a methodology that can be used effectively to evaluate the growth of one's mission/work from time to time and to reorient oneself and the group as found necessary to produce better results and to achieve the set targets.

The Growth Orientation Methodology involves asking two sets of 3 questions and finding satisfactory answers to them in relation to one's mission/goal. Hence, this is also termed '3-Q Methodology'.

The two sets of 3 questions are:

A1. Where are we?

A2. Why are we here?

A3. What are we going to do next?

B1. How are we going to do it?

B2. Who is going to do it?

B3. When are we going to do it?

Satisfactory answers to the first set of 3 questions will help us to take stock of the situation and understand well the crisis/problem if any. This will in turn enable us to prepare ourselves for a creative response to the crisis/problem at hand.

We need to face every crisis creatively, keeping in mind the truth that hidden within a crisis, there can also be 'seeds of grace' that can provide new opportunities for growth and development. For a person of faith, every failure can also be a steppingstone and every crisis can also be an opportunity for further growth. Disciples of Sadguru Jesus Christ are called to be such persons of faith.

Satisfactory answers to the second set of 3 questions will enable us to solve the problem/manage the crisis effectively. Delegating responsibility and demanding accountability with clearly defined terms of reference are very important requirements in every crisis-management /problem-solving effort.

The natural law that a 'committee of mothers will never deliver a baby' is to be always kept in mind. It is always one mother who conceives and delivers the baby. Others can only help. This law of nature holds good in our private and public life.

Every creative effort begins with one individual or a very small group of like-minded individuals. Hence, in a society/nation/religion, where the dignity and freedom of the individual human person are not respected, there will be virtually no creativity. Such a society/nation/religion tends to become status-quoist, traditional and repetitive. All wise and spiritually-inclined persons are expected to keep these truths in mind and act accordingly.

Constituent – 11

The Peace of Christ Meditation

Over the years of my *sadhana* and *tapasya*, I have developed an Inner Peace Meditation termed *'Shanti Yajna'* to improve one's physical, mental and spiritual health. This Meditation is based on the four socio-spiritual pillars of forgiveness, reconciliation, gratitude and self-surrender inspired by the living Spirit of Christ. This Meditation is also made a constituent element of the 'Indian face of the Christian faith'.

The *'Shanti Yajna'* Meditation is our core spiritual exercise. It is also termed 'Inner Peace Meditation'. However, it is more popularly known as 'Peace of Christ Meditation', because the socio-spiritual 'gifts' of forgiveness, reconciliation, gratitude and self-surrender are received by us from the eternally loving and ever-compassionate Parent God in, with. and through the Christ-Spirit. It is also known as 'New Creation Meditation' because it can help to make us 'new creations' in Christ through forgiveness, reconciliation, gratitude and self-surrender.

'Christ-Spirit' is the Spirit of forgiveness, reconciliation, gratitude and self-surrender given to humanity by Divine Providence in, with, and through Sadguru Jesus Christ. Just as one need not become a British citizen to listen to BBC News, one also need not become a 'baptized' Christian to receive the Christ-Spirit of forgiveness, reconciliation, gratitude and self-surrender. All people of goodwill can receive the Christ-Spirit by willingly and consciously accepting Sadguru Jesus Christ as the Lord and Master of their hearts and lives. There is no need for any religious conversion or cultural alienation to receive the Christ-Spirit and to practice the Peace of Christ Meditation.

1.   The Four Stages of Peace of Christ Meditation

The Peace of Christ Meditation has four stages. These are:

Stage – 1: *Stage of Acceptance* - This is the stage of accepting the living Spirit of Christ into one's life without religious conversion and cultural alienation.

Process: Breathe in deeply saying *'Yesoo'* silently in the mind (We are accepting the living Spirit of Sadguru Jesus Christ into our hearts and lives). Breathe out gently saying *'Shanti'* silently in the mind (We are sending out the peace of Christ to the world). Do this for a few minutes.

Stage – 2: *Stage of Forgiveness & Reconciliation* - This is the stage of forgiveness and reconciliation in and through the living Spirit of Christ. We need to forgive people their offences committed against us. We also need to seek forgiveness from those against whom we have committed any offence. Further, we need to forgive ourselves. Above all, we need to reconcile with God, the eternally loving and ever compassionate and forgiving Parent of all humankind, through repentance for all our 'sins' of commissions and omissions that have alienated us from divine grace and from one another.

Process: Recollect the faces of individuals towards whom we have any anger, hatred, and such other negative feelings. Pray for them and bless them in the name of Sadguru Jesus Christ. Repeat this process also for those who may have negative feelings towards us. Repeat the process for our own selves also by recollecting the incidents that made us feel ashamed of ourselves, or angry with ourselves. Forgive ourselves in the name of Sadguru Jesus Christ. Seek forgiveness from God in the name of Sadguru Jesus Christ for all our 'sins' of commissions and omissions.

Stage – 3: *Stage of Gratitude* - This is the stage for us to express our gratitude for all the blessings that we have received from God.

Process: Thank God for all those who have helped us become what we are today, beginning with our own parents, siblings, spouse and children. Above all, we need to thank and praise God for the gift of Sadguru Jesus Christ, as 'the way, the truth and the life' for us in our quest for the meaning and purpose of life in this world and thereafter. An attitude of gratitude will bring abundance of divine blessings into our lives.

Stage – 4: *Stage of total self-surrender* - This is the stage of total self-surrender to God in, with, and through the living Spirit of Christ following the example of Sadguru Jesus Christ.

Process: Surrender our inner beings, our bodies, our relationships, our environment, and all that we have and we are, to God in, with, and through the living spirit of Christ to be purified and sanctified by His Holy Spirit. Be still and silent. Open our hearts and minds fully to the living Spirit of Christ. We will then feel as if we are gently being led to an ever deeper experience of the abiding love, peace and joy of Christ, and to the unitive spiritual consciousness of our oneness with God, the Ultimate Reality. We can then bless others with the divine love, peace, and joy of Christ that we have come to receive and experience through this meditation.

The Shanti Yajna Meditation/Peace of Christ Meditation/ New Creation Meditation will enable one to be joyful, peaceful, and loving. It will also develop an abiding Unitive Eco-Spiritual Consciousness in those who practice it regularly. This Unitive Eco-Spiritual Consciousness will develop in us the much-needed Collective Eco-Spiritual Responsibility which is a basic requirement for a culture of love, peace, and sustainable development to emerge in the pandemic-devastated world.

Constituent – 12

Fruitful Christian Life

The 12th Constituent of the 'Indian face of the Christian faith' is a five-point 'way of life' following which one can live one's Christian faith in the pandemic-devastated and violence-ridden world freely, happily, peacefully, and fruitfully without religious conversion and cultural alienation. Following this five-point 'way of life' one can grow continuously in one's spiritual quest and divine life in this world as an authentic disciple of Sadguru Jesus Christ. This five-point 'fruitful Christian life' is also termed *'Pancha Dharma'*. It can also be termed a five-point 'Rule of life' for authentic Christian discipleship.

The five 'Rules of life' of authentic Christian discipleship constituting the *'Pancha Dharma'* are briefly explained below.

1. *Prarthana* (Prayer): We, the disciples of Sadguru Jesus Christ are called to be men and women of prayer. We can pray in our own places, in our own ways, and at our own times following the manner of prayer taught by our Divine Master (Matt 6: 5-14). True prayer is being grateful to God for the gift of life and for the gift of the Earth Family of which we human beings and all other living beings are members. It is also the ability to see the living presence of God in the hearts of all people and in

the whole Earth Family. We, the disciples of the Divine Master, are also called to enjoy the 'Peace of Christ' which the world cannot give or take away from us. We can enjoy this 'Peace of Christ' which is beyond human understanding by being united to the living Spirit of Christ, our Divine Master, through the Peace of Christ Meditation that is included as Constituent – 11 above. We can practice this Meditation individually or collectively every day at a specific time and place in order to receive maximum benefit from it.

2.   *Padhana* (Study): We are called to study well and be rooted in the Constituents of the 'Indian face of the Christian faith'. We also need to read and reflect regularly on the four 'Gospels' included in the New Testament, especially on the 'Gospel according to John' which is often referred to as the 'Gospel for India'. We are required to strive continuously to deepen our experience and to expand our knowledge of God and His Christ. This is 'eternal life' (John 17: 3). We have to further develop the much-needed Unitive Eco-Spiritual Consciousness through regular studies, reflections, and practices so that we can live in total harmony and peace with all members of the Earth Family.

3.   *Pravarthana* (Action): Disciples of Sadguru Jesus Christ have to be men and women of courageous and selfless action to rebuild the pandemic-devastated and violence-ridden world on the strong foundation of the 'Indian face of the Christian faith' without religious conversion and cultural alienation. The various initiatives presented in Part-Three of this book are meant to provide such opportunities and programmes to interested people. In the multi-religious context of India, we also should strive tirelessly and fearlessly to protect and promote the Constitutional values of Justice, Liberty, Equality

and Fraternity, and the Fundamental Duties of Indian citizens.

4. *Prabodhana* (Instruction): Disciples of Sadguru Jesus Christ should always be prepared to instruct and guide interested people on the 'Indian face of the Christian faith' and on the 'Gospel of love and peace' of Lord Jesus Christ.

5. *Protsahana* (Encouragement): Every disciple of the Divine Master should appreciate, encourage, and support all peace-loving people of goodwill in the world from all religious/cultural backgrounds who are working selflessly for promoting the 'Kingdom of God' (*Dharma Rajya*) of love, righteousness, peace and reconciliation on earth.

We will find that adherence to this five-point Way/Rule of Christian life will enable us to lead happy, healthy, peaceful and fruitful lives in this world as disciples of the Divine Master without religious conversion and cultural alienation.

*　　*　　*　　*　　*　　*　　*　　*

'Dharma Bharathi Darsana Samhita'

The 'Indian face of the Christian faith' with its twelve Constituents will constitute a new School of Thought termed *'Dharma Bharathi Darsana Samhita'*.

The Sanskrit root *'Bha'* implies light. The word *'Rathi'* implies one who drives a *Ratha* (chariot). The term *'Bharathi'* here implies the Power (Force) or the Person driving the chariot of light. The word 'Dharma' is used by us here to mean 'Righteousness'. Hence, the term *'Dharma Bharathi'* implies the Power (Force) or the Person driving the chariot of 'Light of Righteousness' in this world.

'Mother India' is accepted and presented by us as the 'Power' (Force) driving the chariot of 'Light of Righteousness' in this world. Sadguru Jesus Christ is accepted and presented by us as the Person/ Divine Master driving the chariot of 'Light of Righteousness' in this world. Mother India and Sadguru Jesus Christ have been the 'two loves' of my heart ever since my first personal encounter with the living Spirit of Christ in the Air Force Hospital, Bangaluru, in 1982. All my initiatives ever since then have been physical expressions of an ongoing effort for an integration of these two loves of my heart into a life-transforming mission of my 'second life'.

The term *'Dharma Bharathi'* is used by us here to imply an integration of the Power/Force (Mother India) and the Person/

Divine Master (Sadguru Jesus Christ) driving the chariot of 'Light of Righteousness' in this world. The 'Indian face of the Christian faith' is an Integral School of Thought born from a 'spiritual marriage' of 'Mother India' (the Force/Power driving the chariot of righteousness) and Sadguru Jesus Christ (the Person/Divine Master driving the chariot of righteousness) that has taken place in my 'second life'. I have termed this School of Thought 'Dharma Bharathi Darsana Samhita'. (The term 'Darshana Samhita' here implies a 'School of Thought'). The twelve Constituents of the 'Indian face of the Christian faith' presented above will also constitute the twelve elements of this 'Dharma Bharathi' School of Thought/ 'Dharma Bharathi Darsana Samhita'.

'Dharma Bharathi' is also the short form used by us to represent the vision of 'Bharatiya Dharma Rajya' which is the vision of a spiritually awakened, morally regenerated, economically prosperous and politically strong great new India built on the strong foundation of the 'Dharma Bharathi Darsana Samhita'.

'Dharma Bharathi' will be a mother of love and princess of peace in the world family of nations and a disciple nation of God on earth. The 'Dharma Bharathi Darsana Samhita' is a School of Thought that can transform the pandemic-devastated India into a 'Bharatiya Dharma Rajya' / 'Dharma Bharathi' that will shine forth in the world as a 'New Creation in Christ' without religious conversion and cultural alienation.

'Dharma Bharathi Darsana Samhita' is envisaged to be a School of Thought for human solidarity, holistic development and integral peace on earth. 'Human solidarity' implies that humanity is a large family bound with a common destiny. 'Holistic development' implies the physical, intellectual, emotional, spiritual, social, economic, political, religious, scientific, technological, ecological and cultural development of humankind. 'Integral peace' implies that peace which comes from an integration of the personal, social and ecological dimensions of human life in this world.

The '*Dharma Bharathi*' School of Thought will help to spiritualize Christianity and usher in the 'second stage' in the redemptive mission of Sadguru Jesus Christ in this world.

The first stage in the redemptive mission of Sadguru Jesus Christ was the stage of institutionalization of the Christian Faith. This had begun with the declaration of Christianity as the 'Official Religion' of the Roman Empire under Emperor Constantine.

The second stage of the redemptive mission of Sadguru Jesus Christ will be the stage of ushering in a culture of love, peace and sustainable development on earth through an 'Integrated World Order' built on the '*Dharma Bharathi*' School of Thought for human solidarity, holistic development and integral peace.

The COVID-19 pandemic marks the end of the 'first stage' and the beginning of the 'second stage' in the redemptive mission of Sadguru Jesus Christ, the incarnation in human history of *Prabhu Parameshwar*, the one triune God of Divine Light – Divine Love – Divine Spirit. Kerala, the cradle of the Christian Faith in the Indian subcontinent, is called to be cradle and seedbed of this second stage in the redemptive mission of Sadguru Jesus Christ.

*   *   *   *   *   *   *   *

The Tree of *'Dharma Bharathi'*

The twelve Constituents of the 'Indian face of the Christian faith'/ *'Dharma Bharathi Darsana Samhita'* presented above can be divided into five groups. Together they will form a Tree of *'Dharma Bharathi'*. Constituent-1 ('Unbound Christ') and Constituent-2 ('Open Christianity') form group-1. This group is like the roots of the Tree of *'Dharma Bharathi'*.

Constituent – 3 ('Interreligious Theology'), Constituent – 4 ('Advaitic Christology') and Constituent-5 ('Inclusive Missiology') form group-2. This group is like the trunk of the Tree of *'Dharma Bharathi'*.

Constituent-6 ('Liberative Spirituality'), Constituent-7 ('Holistic Philosophy') and Constituent-8 ('Eco-Spiritual Ideology') form group-3. This group is like the branches of the Tree of *'Dharma Bharathi'*.

Constituent-9 ('Enlightened Christian leadership') and Constituent-10 ('Christian Mission Methodologies') form group-4. This group is like the leaves and flowers of the Tree of *'Dharma Bharathi'*.

Constituent-11 ('Peace of Christ Meditation') and Constituent -12 ('Fruitful Christian life') form group-5. This group is like the fruits of the Tree of *'Dharma Bharathi'*

*   *   *   *   *   *   *   *

The verdict of history will be passed and the destiny of humankind will be determined by the courage, wisdom, creativity and perseverance with which the disciples of Sadguru Jesus Christ in the pandemic-devastated and violence-ridden world pursue and promote the 'Indian face of the Christian faith' / *'Dharma Bharathi Darsana Samhita'.*

PART – THREE

INTEGRAL RENAISSANCE OF INDIA

Introduction ... 169

1. Navasrushti International ... 172

2. The Integral Renaissance of India ... 178

3. Christusishya Shanti Sangham ... 180

4. Dharma Bharathi Institutes ... 183

5. Dharma Bharathi Mission ... 186

6. Dharma Rajya Vedi ... 188

7. Tyagarchana Shanti Mission ... 191

Appendix A: In Search of the Common Aspects
in Christianity and Hinduism ... 210

Appendix B: Viswa Shanti Peetam ... 225

Introduction

Rebuilding the pandemic-devastated and violence-ridden world on the strong foundation of the 'Indian face of the Christian faith'/ *'Dharma Bharathi Darshana Samhita'* presented in Part-Two of this book will be the most challenging and exciting divine mission ahead of the disciples of Sadguru Jesus Christ in the world during the next few centuries. This global mission of the millennium has to begin from India with the Indian Church.

The disciples of Sadguru Jesus Christ in India will have to work tirelessly, fearlessly, prayerfully and incessantly to bring about an Integral Renaissance of India based on the *'Dharma Bharathi Darshana Samhita'* presented earlier. Such an Integral Renaissance of India will empower this ancient land of religions to be an instrument of God for ushering in a culture of love, peace, and sustainable development in the world.

We have seen elsewhere in this book that India and the Indian Church have important roles to play in rebuilding the pandemic-devastated and violence-ridden world on an eco-spiritual peace and sustainable development paradigm. We have also seen that a peace and sustainable development paradigm based on a scientific Unitive Eco-Spiritual Consciousness will be India's greatest contribution to humanity.

India urgently needs an Integral Renaissance to awaken and empower herself for the mission of the millennium entrusted to her by history and destiny. Such an Integral Renaissance has to bring about a moral and spiritual regeneration of the social, economic, political, religious, and ecological dimensions of India's national life. In the multi-religious context of India, this will have to be an interreligious task.

The Indian Church has an urgent and important mission in bringing about the much-needed Integral Renaissance of India through interreligious cooperative action. The *'Dharma Bharathi Darsana Samhita'* presented in Part-Two will enable the Indian Church to fulfill this urgent and important mission.

An Integral Renaissance of India will awaken and transform India into a *'Bharatiya Dharma Rajya'*, which is the vision of a spiritually awakened, morally regenerated, economically prosperous, and politically strong greater India. The *'Bharatiya Dharma Rajya'* of our vision will be 'a disciple nation of God' to transform the pandemic-devastated and violence-ridden world into a 'New Creation in Christ' without religious conversion and cultural alienation based on the *'Dharma Bharathi Darsana Samhita'*.

*   *   *   *   *   *   *   *

The Part-Three of our book presents the Integral Renaissance of India. This eco-spiritual and interreligious movement was initiated on 30 January 2021. It is being promoted by 'Dharma Rajya Vedi' (DRV) under the legal ownership and accounting authority of a Public Charitable Trust, namely 'Navasrushti International'. Outlines of this Public Charitable Trust and the contents of the 'Commitment to Global Peace' based on which it was founded, are presented in chapter-1.

Chapter-2 presents the outlines of the Integral Renaissance of India. Chapter-3 presents the outlines of an ecumenical communion of disciples of Sadguru Jesus Christ in India termed *'Christusishya Shanti Sangham'* (CSS). Chapter-4 presents the outlines of a network of 'Dharma Bharathi Institutes of Peace & Value Education' (DBIs) to be established by members of CSS to serve as training and orientation institutes to promote the *'Dharma Bharathi Darshana Samhita'* in the world.

Chapter-5 presents the outlines of 'Dharma Bharathi Mission' (DBM) which is an interreligious mission for a poverty-free India (aso a poverty-free world) based on the eco-spiritual ideology of *Tyagarchana* and the '3-E' methodology of 'Education, Employment & Empowerment'.

Chapter-6 presents the outlines of a 'Swadeshi Church' termed 'Dharma Rajya Vedi' (DRV) which is meant to promote the Integral Renaissance of India.

'Chapter-7 presents the outlines of our latest initiative termed 'Tyagarchana Shanti Mission' (TSM) in which all our initiatives are integrated. TSM will provide a strong eco-spiritual and interreligious foundation for the Integral Renaissance of India.

Appendix-A presents an inspiring article by Rev. Dr. Adai Jacob Cor Episcopa that will be very useful for those, who are involved in promoting Hindu-Christian dialogue and joint action for the Integral Renaissance of India.

Appendix-B presents the outlines of the vision of a World Peace Center termed 'Viswa Shanti Peetam'. Comments of some prominent people on 'Viswa Shanti Peetam' are also included in Appendix-B.

1

Navasrushti International

'Navasrushti International' (also known as 'Navasrushti International Trust' or 'NIT') is a Public Charitable Trust founded for national regeneration of India and to help to usher in a civilization of love and culture of peace in the world. NIT was registered in Kerala on 8th September 2005 with a global coverage (Reg. No. IV-97/2005). Dharma Bharathi Ashram established in Mulanthuruthy village near Kochi in 2003 is the Registered Office of NIT which has already won a number of awards for its integrity, transparency, and selfless service rendered to the poor and needy in the country.

The ultimate goal of NIT is to transform the world into a 'New Creation in Christ' (*Navasrushti*) based on the 'Dharma Bharathi' School of Thought for human solidarity, holistic development and integral peace. In the context of NIT the *Dharma Bharathi Darsana Samhita* presented in Part-Two of this book is being referred to as 'Dharma Bharathi' School of Thought for human solidarity, holistic development and integral peace.

NIT was founded and registered in 2005 with the following aim:

'To promote national regeneration of India and help to usher in a civilization of love and culture of peace in the world based on the moral and spiritual values common to all religions by translating into action the 'Commitment to Global Peace' signed by the religious and spiritual leaders of the world at the United Nations in August 2000 at the end of the 'Millennium World Peace Summit of Religious and Spiritual Leaders' through the 'Dharma Bharathi' school of thought for human solidarity, holistic development and integral peace developed and authored by the Settler of this Trust'.

I am the Settler of NIT. I was one of the delegates from India invited by the United Nations for the *'Millennium World Peace Summit of Religious and Spiritual Leaders'* held in New York in August 2000. I was invited in my capacity as the Founder & Acharya-guru of 'Dharma Rajya Vedi' (DRV) & 'Disciples of Christ for Peace' (DCP). I was also one of the signatories to the **'Commitment to Global Peace'** for and on behalf of DRV & DCP.

NIT was registered to promote the vision and action plan of the 'Commitment to Global Peace' based on the *'Dharma Bharathi'* School of Thought developed and authored by its Settler that is now summed up and presented in Part-Two of this book as the 'Indian face of the Christian faith'/ *'Dharma Bharathi Darsana Samhita'*.

The 'Commitment to Global Peace' is given below for easy reference:

Commitment to Global Peace

"Humanity stands at a critical juncture in history, one that calls for strong moral and spiritual leadership to help set a new direction for society. We, as religious and spiritual leaders, recognize our special responsibility for the well-being of the human family and peace on earth.

Whereas the United Nations and the religions of the world have a common concern for human dignity, justice and peace;

Whereas we accept that men and women are equal partners in all aspects of life and children are the hope of the future;

Whereas our religions have contributed to the peace of the world but have also been used to create division and fuel hostilities;

Whereas our world is plagued by violence, war and destruction, which are sometimes perpetrated in the name of religion;

Whereas armed conflict is dire tragedy for the human lives ruined and lost, for the larger living world, and for the future of our religious and spiritual traditions;

Whereas no individual, group or nation can any longer live as an isolated microcosm in our interdependent world, but rather all must realize that our every action has an impact on others and the emerging global community;

Whereas in an interdependent world peace requires agreement on fundamental ethical values;

Whereas there can be no real peace until all groups and communities acknowledge the cultural and religious diversity of the human family in a spirit of mutual respect and understanding;

Whereas building peace requires an attitude of reverence for life, freedom and justice, the eradication of poverty, and the protection of the environment for present and future generations;

Whereas a true culture of peace must be founded upon the cultivation of the inner dimension of peace, which is the heritage of the religious and spiritual traditions;

Whereas religious and spiritual traditions are a core source of the realization of a better life for the human family and all life on Earth;

In the light of the above and with a view to discharging our duty to the human family, we declare our commitment and determination:

1. To collaborate with the United Nations and all men and women of goodwill locally, regionally and globally in the pursuit of peace in all its dimensions;

2. To lead humanity by word and deed in a renewed commitment to ethical and spiritual values, which include a deep sense of respect for all life, for each person's inherent dignity and right to live in a world free of violence;

3. To manage and resolve non-violently the conflicts generated by religious and ethnic differences, and to condemn all violence committed in the name of religion while seeking to remove the roots of the violence;

4. To appeal to all religious communities and ethnic and national groups to respect the right to freedom of religion, to seek reconciliation, and to engage in mutual forgiveness and healing;

5. To awaken in all individuals and communities a sense of shared responsibility for the wellbeing of the human family as a whole and a recognition that all human beings – regardless of religion, race, gender and ethnic origin – have the right to education, health care, and an opportunity to achieve a secure and sustainable livelihood;

6. To promote the equitable distribution of wealth within and among nations, eradicating poverty and reversing the current trend towards a widening gap between rich and poor;

7. To educate our communities about the urgent need to care for the earth's ecological systems and all forms of life and to support to make environmental protection and restoration integral to all development planning and activity;

8. To develop and promote a global reforestation campaign as a concrete and practical means for environmental restoration, calling upon others to join us in regional tree planting programmes;

9. To join with the United Nations in the call for all nation states to work for the universal abolition of nuclear weapons and other weapons of mass destruction for the safety and security of life of this planet;

10. To combat those commercial practices and applications of technology that degrade the environment and the quality of human life;

11. To practice and promote in our communities the values of the inner dimension of peace, including especially study, prayer, meditation, a sense of the sacred, humility, love, compassion, tolerance and a spirit of service, which are fundamental to the creation of a peaceful society.

We, as religious and spiritual leaders, pledge our commitment to work together to promote the inner and outer conditions that foster peace and the nonviolent management and resolution of conflict. We appeal to the followers of all religious traditions and to the human community as a whole to cooperate in building peaceful societies, to seek mutual understanding through dialogue where there are differences, to refrain from violence, to practice compassion, and to uphold the dignity of all life."

*   *   *   *   *   *   *   *

The mission of the era (*Yuga Dharma*) entrusted to NIT by history and destiny is to promote the *'Dharma Bharathi'* School of Thought/ *Dharma Bharathi Darshana Samhita* in the world through various love-inspired initiatives in order to give practical expressions to the

Resolutions included within the 'Commitment to Global Peace' for the implementation of which the religious and spiritual leaders of the world assembled at the United Nations for the Millennium World Peace Summit had declared their commitment and determination.

The following chapters present the important initiatives that are being promoted by NIT to realize its mission and fulfill its *Yuga Dharma*. The last chapter presents our latest initiative termed 'Tyagarchana Shanti Mission' (TSM) in which all initiatives under NIT are integrated for a culture of love, peace and sustainable development in the pandemic-devastated and violence-ridden world. Kerala is taken as a 'pilot project' of NIT & TSM for this purpose.

NIT functions as an open network of Autonomous Regional Units with five or more members based on its Registered Trust Deed.

A seven-member National Board of Trustees elected every three years supervises the activities of NIT and provides the necessary policy guidelines for its members and Regional Units in India.

A 'Navasrushti Academy of Integral Leadership' (NAIL) was started by NIT in 2015 to train its members and leaders.

(NB: For further details of NIT, please refer to its Registered Trust Deed (Reg. No. IV-97/2005) and its Annual Reports. One is also invited to visit the Website of NIT: www.navasrushti.org)

2

The Integral Renaissance of India

'Integral Renaissance of India' implies a moral and spiritual regeneration of the social, economic, political, religious and ecological dimensions of India's national life based on the 'Indian face of the Christian faith'/ *'Dharma Bharathi Darshana Samhita'*.

A 'Swadeshi Church' termed 'Dharma Rajya Vedi' (DRV) (presented in chapter-6 below) will make the Integral Renaissance of India its most important 'Collective Eco-Spiritual Responsibility' (CESR). The book 'Integral Renaissance of India' released by Sri. Arif Mohammad Khan, the Hon. Governor of Kerala, on 14 October 2021 will serve as the 'mission manual' of DRV for its CESR mission.

The Integral Renaissance of India will awaken and transform India into a *'Bharatiya Dharma Rajya'*, which is the vision of a spiritually awakened, morally regenerated, economically prosperous, and politically strong greater India.

'Bharatiya Dharma Rajya' will be 'a disciple nation of God' to transform the pandemic-devastated and violence-ridden world into a 'New Creation in Christ' without religious conversion and cultural alienation based on the *'Dharma Bharathi Darsana Samhita'*.

The living Spirit of Christ will have to provide the 'soul force' to the Integral Renaissance of India. This will require an ecumenical communion of disciples of Sadguru Jesus Christ who are fully dedicated to the mission of the Integral Renaissance of India inspired by the concepts of 'creative fidelity' and 'collective eco-spiritual responsibility'. *'Christusishya Shanti Sangham'* (CSS) presented in the following chapter is meant to be such an ecumenical communion.

'Peace & Value Education' is the basis of peaceful social transformation and value-based nation-building. Well-qualified and highly motivated members of CSS will establish a network of 'Dharma Bharathi Institutes' of Peace & Value Education (DBIs) in India to educate 'We, the People of India' on the *'Dharma Bharathi Darsana Samhita'*.

Economic well-being and sustainable development are basic prerequisites for the emergence of a civilization of love and a culture of peace in the world. 'Dharma Bharathi Mission' (DBM) presented in chapter-5 will work towards this goal.

A 'Swadeshi Chruch' is needed for the Integral Renaissance of India based on the 'Indian face of the Christian faith'/ *'Dharma Bharathi Darshana Samhita'*. 'Dharma Rajya Vedi' (DRV) presented in chapter-6 is meant to serve as such a 'Swadeshi Church' without religious conversion and cultural alienation.

The 'Tyagarchana Shanti Mission' (chapter-7) is being promoted by DRV to provide a strong eco-spiritual foundation for the Integral Renaissance of India.

3

Christusishya Shanti Sangham

'Christusishya Shanti Sangham' (CSS) is envisaged to be a fully dedicated communion of disciples of Sadguru Jesus Christ who are 'consecrated' to God in Christ for the Integral Renaissance of India based on the 'Indian face of the Christian faith'/ *'Dharma Bharathi Darsana Samhita'* without religious conversion and cultural alienation.

'Disciples of Christ for Peace' (DCP) was founded in 1998 by us to serve as a 'Consecrated Society' for 'Unity and Peace in India through *Sahana Yoga*' based on the Fundamental Duties of Indian citizens given under Article: 51-A of the Indian Constitution. The late Most Rev. Samineni Arulappa, the then Archbishop of Hyderabad, was the Co-Founder & first Patron of DCP.

DCP has undergone a number of modifications in its evolutionary growth over the years. It was also registered in Kerala as a Public Charitable Trust in 2009 with a global coverage (Reg. No. IV-72/2009). DCP was reoriented and reorganized under its Malayalam name *'Christusishya Shanti Sangham'* (CSS) with the release and dedication to God of my semi-autobiographical book titled 'A New Creation in Christ' on 08 July 2020.

CSS will hereafter function as a 'National Ecumenical Communion' of fully dedicated disciples of Sadguru Jesus Christ who are 'consecrated' to God in Christ for the mission of promoting the Integral Renaissance of India based on the 'Indian face of the Christian faith'/ *'Dharma Bharathi Darsana Samhita'* presented in Part-Two of this book. Members of CSS will strive tirelessly, fearlessly, prayerfully, and incessantly to put into practice all 12 Constituents of the 'Indian face of the Christian faith' / *'Dharma Bharathi Darsana Samhita'* in their own lived-life contexts.

The 'Dharma Bharathi School of Forgiveness & Reconciliation' (DBSFR) founded in 2006 under the legal ownership of NIT will be responsible to provide the necessary training and orientation for aspiring members of CSS.

Members of CSS will hereafter live and function in accordance with its new Constitution adopted with effect from Pentecost 2021 (23 May 2021). This new Constitution of CSS is presented in chapter-6a of the book 'Integral Renaissance of India'. However, this book in your hands is to be accepted as the final 'mission manual' of CSS as what is written in this book supersedes all that is written by me on the same subject in any other book earlier.

CSS will function under the legal ownership and accounting authority of NIT (Reg. No. IV-97/2005).

Members of CSS hereafter will also provide the necessary soul force and inner spiritual dynamism to NIT and to all initiatives under the legal ownership and accounting authority of NIT, by serving as the 'salt of the earth and light of the world' within them.

The founder of CSS (DCP) was a signatory to the 'Commitment to Global Peace' signed at the United Nations by religious and spiritual leaders of the world in August 2000. Members of CSS will ever remain committed to the Resolutions included in the 'Commitment to Global Peace'.

(NB: For further details of CSS please refer to chapters 6 & 6a of the book 'Integral Renaissance of India' and to Chapter-8 of the book 'A New Creation in Christ'.)

4

Dharma Bharathi Institutes

'Dharma Bharathi Institutes of Peace & Value Education' (DBIs) are envisaged to be Autonomous Local Institutes established by well-qualified and highly motivated members of CSS in India and other countries to promote the 'Indian face of the Christian faith'/ *Dharma Bharathi Darsana Samhita*' for ushering in a culture of love, peace and sustainable development in the pandemic-devastated and violence-ridden world.

The 'Dharma Bharathi National Institute of Peace & Value Education' (DBNI) started in 1993 at Indore in MP will serve as a Coordinating Center for DBIs in India. DBNI is presently functioning from Lucknow, UP, with Dr. S K Singh serving as its Director General.

All DBIs in India will be affiliated to DBNI. The DBIs along with the DBNI will form a 'Dharma Bharathi National Open University' of Peace & Value Education (DBNOU) in India in course of time.

DBIs will also be established in other countries by members of CSS to promote the 'Indian face of the Christian faith' /*Dharma Bharathi Darsana Samhita*'.

The various DBNOUs established in different countries will be linked up together to form a 'Dharma Bharathi Global Open University' (DBGOU) of Peace & Value Education in course of time.

The DBGOU will provide a strong educational foundation for rebuilding the pandemic-devastated and violence-ridden world on the strong foundation of the *Dharma Bharathi Darsana Samhita* for establishing an Integrated World Order that will usher in a culture of love, peace, and sustainable development on earth in the fullness of time with divine grace.

DBNI, DBIs, DBNOU & DBGOU will function under the legal ownership and accounting authority of NIT.

*   *   *   *   *   *   *   *

The first objective of the Navasrushti International Trust given under Article- 7a of its Registered Trust Deed is:

"Establishing a Dharma Bharathi Global Open University of Peace and Value Education in the form of a network of Dharma Bharathi Schools of Study and Research, and autonomous Dharma Bharathi Institutes of Peace and Value Education as well as Dharma Bharathi Community Colleges & Schools to promote a civilization of love and a culture of peace in the world based on the *'Dharma Bharathi School of Thought'* for human solidarity, holistic development and integral peace developed and authored by the Settler of the Trust and on the *'Commitment to Global Peace'* signed at the United Nations by the religious and spiritual leaders of the world at the end of the *'Millennium World Peace Summit of Religious and Spiritual Leaders'* organized in New York in August 2000, and collaborating with the United Nations and other like-minded agencies for this purpose."

A 'Viswa Shanti Peetam' (World Peace Center) as presented in Appendix-B to this book will be established at a suitable location in India by NIT to serve as the Global Headquarters and Coordination Center for the proposed DBGOU.

(NB: For further details of DBGOU and the proposed World Peace Center, please refer to the book 'Viswa Shanti Peetam' released on 14 October 2021 by Sri. Arif Mohammad Khan, Hon. Governor of Kerala, at Gandhi Park, Thiruvananthapuram, Kerala.)

5

Dharma Bharathi Mission

The 'Dharma Bharathi Mission' (DBM) was originally founded on 30 January 2003 at Hyderabad as a network of teachers trained by DBNI for national regeneration of India.

An all-India tour termed *'Desh Vandana-2007'* was undertaken by us from 30 January 2007 to 30 January 2008, calling for a 'Second Freedom Struggle' with the goal and motto *'hunger-free, caste-free and corruption-free India'*.

Following the *Desh Vandana-2007,* DBM was reoriented and reorganized as an interreligious organization for a 'hunger-free, caste-free, and corruption-free India'. However, during the first Annual Convention of the Second Freedom Struggle of India organized by DBM at Sevagram Ashram, Wardha, on 29-31 January 2009, it was resolved that DBM would concentrate its efforts on achieving the first goal of 'hunger-free India'. It was also resolved that DBM would begin its 'hunger-free India' campaign from the slums of Mumbai.

DBM has developed and applied effectively a 3-E methodology to achieve its aim. This 3-E methodology consists of 'Education-Employment-Empowerment'. This 3-E methodology was originally developed and applied in Kerala a century ago by Sree Narayana Guru, the great spiritual leader who had proclaimed *'One Caste, One Religion & One God for Humankind'*. He had also convened the first Interreligious Parliament in Asia. The 3-E methodology was developed and applied by him effectively for the integral development of his downtrodden Ezhava community which has become a great political and economic power in Kerala today. DBM has adopted and made its own this effective 3-E methodology for building a 'Poverty-free India'.

DBM has already won several awards for its selfless and dedicated service for the development of the poor and downtrodden youth and women in the slums of Mumbai.

Sri. Paramjeet Singh, a dynamic IRS officer, serves as the National President of DBM. His own personal motto *'Give till it hurts'* is also adopted as the motto of DBM. He has built up an effective and efficient 'Team DBM' to carry forward the historic task of building a 'Poverty-free India' based on the ideology of *Tyagarchana* through the 3-E methodology.

DBM will continue to serve and grow as an interreligious organization for a 'Poverty-free India' leading to a 'Poverty-free world' based on the ideology of *Tyagarchana* through the 3-E methodology. DBM will also continue to function under the legal ownership and accounting authority of NIT.

NAIL will be responsible to provide the necessary training and orientation for members and leaders of DBM.

DRV will provide the necessary organizational support and CSS will provide the necessary 'soul force' to DBM.

(NB: For further details of DBM please refer to the Annual Reports of NIT and visit URL: www.dbmindia.org)

Dharma Rajya Vedi

Ever since my first personal encounter with the living Spirit of Christ in 1982 I have been on a pilgrimage of faith. I have also been in a spiritual quest to integrate my Christ-experience with my deep love for my motherland. Sadguru Jesus Christ and Mother India have been the 'two loves' of my heart. My spiritual quest and pilgrimage of faith have been aimed at an integration of these two loves of my heart into one life-transforming mission. 'Dharma Raya Vedi' (DRV) is the fruit of this spiritual quest and pilgrimage of faith. DRV is the vision of a 'Swadeshi Church' built on the strong foundation of the 'Indian face of the Christian faith'/*Dharma Bharathi Darshana Samhita*' presented in Part-Two of this book without religious conversion and cultural alienation.

DRV was founded on 02 October 1990 at Kochi in Kerala as an Interreligious Organization for a New Indian Renaissance based on an integral vision of life and reality and a synthesis of science and spirituality. I was a signatory for and on behalf of DRV to the 'Commitment to Global Peace' signed at the United Nations by religious and spiritual leaders of the world in August 2000. NIT was founded and registered on 08 September 2005 in order to give practical expression to the contents of the 'Commitment to Global

Peace' in the multi-religious and multi-cultural context of India. DRV has been pursuing this goal of NIT ever since.

DRV has undergone a number of modifications over the years of its evolutionary growth. A new Constitution was adopted for DRV with effect from 23 May 2021. This new Constitution of DRV is presented in chapter-5a of the book 'Integral Renaissance of India' which also now serves as its 'mission manual'.

With the publication of this book in your hands, DRV is being further reoriented and reorganized as a 'Swadeshi Church' in the form of a 'National Eco-Spiritual & Interreligious Organization'. DRV will function as a network of autonomous local CESR communities termed 'Dharma Rajya Satsangs' consisting of 3 to 33 members inspired to live by the *Dharma Bharathi Darsana Samhita*'. Members of DRV will be committed to the mission of promoting the Integral Renaissance of India based on its mission manual. They will accept and commit themselves to this historic mission as their Collective Eco-Spiritual Responsibility (CESR).

DRV presently has an ad hoc National Coordinating Team with Ambassador K P Fabian, IFS (Retd) serving as its National President. The ad hoc National Coordinating Office of DRV presently functions from Lucknow. The Kerala State Coordinating Office of DRV functions from Dharma Bharathi Ashram, Mulanthuruthy, Kochi-682314. The proposed 'Viswa Shanti Peetam' (Appendix-B) will serve as the permanent Headquarters of DRV which will also expand its mission to other parts of the world in course of time with divine grace.

Every 'Dharma Rajya Satsang' will be an autonomous 'CESR community' by its nature, administration, and function as outlined in the new Constitution of DRV. Members of DRV will adopt and live according to this new Constitution presented in chapter-5a of its mission manual. However, this book in your hands will serve as the final authority in matters connected with the vision and mission of DRV. Navasrushti Academy of Integral Leadership (NAIL) will be responsible to provide the necessary training and orientation for members of DRV. CSS presented in chapter-3 will provide the necessary soul force and inner spiritual dynamism to this 'Swadeshi Church' which will function under the legal ownership and accounting authority of NIT.

(NB: For further details about DRV, please refer to chapters 5 & 5a of its mission manual titled 'Integral Renaissance of India'.)

7

Tyagarchana Shanti Mission

'Tyagarchana Shanti Mission' (TSM) was originally initiated in Uttar Pradesh during 2014-2017 as a movement for promoting communal harmony and interreligious cooperation for a culture of peace. The unprecedented communal violence in Muzaffarnagar District in western UP during August-September 2013 was the motivation for us to initiate TSM.

A six-month long *Tyagarchana Shanti Yatra* was undertaken by us across UP during August 2015 - January 2016 for promoting communal harmony and interreligious cooperation in the State.

A cultural troupe named 'Prerana Kala Manch' from Banares under the leadership of Rev. Fr. Anand Mathew, IMS, accompanied us in the *Tyagarchana Shanti Yatra*. Prerana Kala Manch presented more than 200 cultural programmes during the six-month long *Tyagarchana Shanti Yatra* across UP to educate the public on the need and urgency for communal harmony and interreligious cooperation for a culture of peace in India.

The entire expense for the six-month long *Tyagarchana Shanti Yatra*, including payments for the artists of Prerana Kala Manch and petrol for vehicles (Total expense= Rs. 16. 5 lakhs), was met from the *Tyagarchana* contributions received from the generous supporters of the programmes during the *Yatra* in UP.

An interreligious campaign termed 'Hunger-free Childhood Campaign' (*Bhookmukt Bachpan Abhiyaan*) was also initiated in Lucknow at the end of the six-month long *Tyagarchana Shanti Yatra*. Two Ashrams ('Kabir Bharathi Ashram' at Jaitanpur & 'Viswa Shanti Vidya Peetam Ashram' at Lucknow) are also established in UP following the *Tyagarchana Shanti Yatra*. The land, buildings, and funds for these ashrams also came as *Tyagarchana* contributions from peace-loving people of goodwill in UP.

A two-day Interreligious Parliament for world peace termed '*Viswa Shanti Sansad-2017*' was organized under the banner of Tyagarchana Shanti Mission on 04 - 05 of August 2017 at Patna, Bihar. A campaign termed '*Khushhaal Bachpan Abhiyaan*' (Happy Childhood Campaign) was initiated as a 'follow up action plan' by the participants of '*Viswa Shanti Sansad-2017*'. This was a modified version of the 'Hunger-free Childhood Campaign' (*Bhookmukt Bachpan Abhiyaan*) that was initiated in Lucknow at the end of the six-month long *Tyagarchana Shanti Yatra*. The entire expense for '*Viswa Shanti Sansad-2017*' also came from generous *Tyagarchana* contributions from peace-loving people of goodwill from different religious traditions.

*   *   *   *   *   *   *   *

Following the outbreak of COVID-19 pandemic, TSM is being given a new orientation with a new content by DRV. With effect from 21 September 2021 (21 September is celebrated as the 'International Day of Peace' by the United Nations every year) TSM is being transformed into '*An Eco-Spiritual Mission & Interreligious Movement for a Culture of Love, Peace, & Sustainable Development in the Pandemic-devastated World, beginning from and with Kerala*' inspired by the theme of the International Day of Peace 2021 which was **"Recovering better for an equitable and sustainable world".** An interreligious prayer meeting was organized in Dharma Bharathi Ashram by DRV on 21 September 2021 to dedicate the reoriented and reorganized TSM to God and humanity.

DRV was also rededicated to God and humanity on 21 September 2021 in Dharma Bharathi Ashram as an 'Eco-Spiritual and Interreligious Organization' committed to work with UN and all other organizations and institutions in the world for a culture of love, peace, and sustainable development in the pandemic-devastated world. The Founder of DRV was a signatory to the 'Commitment to Global Peace' signed at the United Nations by the religious and spiritual leaders of the world in the *'Millennium World Peace Summit of Religious and Spiritual Leaders'* in August 2000. He had signed the 'Commitment to Global Peace' in that Millennium World Peace Summit for and on behalf of DRV & DCP. (Ref. chapter-1 above).

A week-long *Sarva Dharma Sadbhavana Kerala Yatra* was undertaken in Kerala from 08 October to 14 October 2021 to promote communal harmony and interreligious cooperation for a culture of peace in the State under the spiritual leadership of DRV. The *Yatra* concluded on 14 October 2021 with a day-long fasting at Gandhi Park, Thiruvananthapuram. The Hon. Governor of Kerala, Sri Arif Mohammad Khan, was the Chief Guest in the concluding function of the *Yatra*. He also inaugurated *'Tyagarchana Mahayajnam'* as a three-tier comprehensive interreligious action programme of DRV for a culture of love, peace, and sustainable development in Kerala.

Following the *Sarva Dharma Sadbhavana Kerala Yatra*, TSM was reorganized based on the comprehensive action plan of DRV that was inaugurated by the Hon. Governor of Kerala on 14 October.

A two-day Interreligious Parliament termed '*Sarva Dharma Shanti Sangamam 2021*' was organized by DRV at YMCA, Aluva on 10 & 11 December 2021 for this purpose.

TSM was transformed into an eco-spiritual mission as well as an interreligious movement for a culture of love, peace, and sustainable development in the pandemic-devastated world beginning from and with Kerala in the two-day '*Sarva Dharma Shanti Sangamam*'. The inclusive vision and the eco-spiritual ideology of DRV presented in its mission manual and its 3-tier comprehensive action plan inaugurated on 14 October 2021 by the Hon. Governor of Kerala were incorporated as the vision, ideology, and action plan of TSM in this two-day Interreligious Parliament.

The transformed TSM was formally inaugurated in the '*Sarva Dharma Shanti Sangamam*' by Hon. Justice Kurian Joseph, former Judge of the Supreme Court of India.

DRV is the 'Promoter' of the transformed TSM which functions under the legal ownership of NIT. A 'mission manual' is published for TSM by NIT. It was dedicated to God and humanity in Dharma Bharathi Ashram on 30 January 2022 by Dr. Kuriakose Mor Theophilose Metropolitan (President, Ecumenical Commission, Malankara Jacobite Syrian Orthodox Church; Resident Metropolitan & Professor, MSOTS; and Chairman, National Council of Mentors, DRV). This mission manual contains the vision, ideology, action plan, organization and leadership of TSM, and the outlines of a proposed 20-year Kerala pilot project of TSM. It also includes the conditions for like-minded organizations and institutions to collaborate with DRV/NIT for achieving the aim and objectives of TSM and its Kerala pilot project.

TSM will lay a strong eco-spiritual foundation for the Integral Renaissance of India. Kerala is adopted by NIT & DRV as the seedbed and inspirational model of TSM. A twenty-year 'Kerala pilot project' was also initiated during the two-day Interreligious Parliament to transform Kerala into a *'Chaitanya Keralam'*, which will be an inspirational role model of a culture of love, peace, and sustainable development in the pandemic-devastated world.

Transforming Kerala into a *Chaitanya Keralam* of love, peace, and sustainable development is the divine mission of the millennium (*Yuga Dharma*) entrusted to NIT & DRV by history and destiny through the 20-year Kerala pilot project.

TSM will have four constituent organizations - Tyagarchana Yuva Shakti (TYS), Tyagarchana Mathru Shakti (TMS), Tyagarchana Pitru Shakti (TPS) & Tyagarchana Guru Shakti (TGS) - as outlined in its mission manual under chapters 3D & 3E. Out of these four constituent organizations, TYS will be the 'Task Force' to achieve the aim and objectives of TSM. DRV will promote TSM and its Kerala pilot project according to the mission manual of TSM.

A cadre of enlightened teacher-leaders termed 'Tyagarchana Acharya Parishad' (TAP) and a network of 'Tyagarchana Shanti Bhavans' (TSBs) will be established by DRV under the legal ownership of NIT to promote the aim and objectives of TSM and its Kerala pilot project.

*   *   *   *   *   *   *   *

A.   Tyagarchana Acharya Parishad (TAP)

'Enlightened leadership' is a basic requirement for the success of any mission. TSM needs a cadre of enlightened teacher-leaders who are committed and determined to serve as visionary-missionaries of TSM for promoting its vision, ideology, and action plan among the people, especially among the youth and students.

'Tyagarchana Acharya Parishad' (TAP) is being created by DRV as a cadre of well-trained and highly motivated teacher-leaders and visionary-missionaries, who are committed to the divine task of providing enlightened leadership to TSM and make it bear abundant fruits for the glory of God and good of humanity.

Members of TAP will strive tirelessly, fearlessly, incessantly, and prayerfully to fulfill their divine mission by giving practical expressions in their own lives to the inclusive vision, eco-spiritual ideology, and comprehensive action plan of TSM as included in its mission manual. Following the Gandhian example, members of TAP will have to 'become the message' that they want to promote in the society. Members of TAP will expand their divine mission to other parts of India (and the world) in course of time.

The five principles of 'Enlightened Christian Leadership' (Constituent-9, Part-Two) will be modified and adopted for TAP as its five 'Enlightened Leadership Principles'.

The three 'Christian Mission Methodologies' (Constituent-10) will be modified as the three 'Appropriate Mission Methodologies'; the 'Peace of Christ Meditation' (Constituent-11) will be modified as 'Inner Peace Meditation'; and the 'Five Rules of Fruitful Christian Life' (Constituent-12) will be modified as the 'Five Rules of Fruitful Life' and adopted for TAP.

The 'Navasrushti Academy of Integral Leadership' (NAIL) started by NIT in 2015 will be responsible to conduct the necessary training programmes for aspiring members of TAP.

B.   Tyagarchana Shanti Bhavans (TSBs)

DRV under the leadership of TAP will strive incessantly, tirelessly, fearlessly and prayerfully for the success of TSM by training, motivating, and guiding the members of Tyagarchana Yuva Shakti

(TYS) to establish a network of 'Tyagarchana Shanti Bhavans' (TSBs) with the following five important common objectives:

1. To serve as 'Centers of Caring Love' to render loving and grateful 'Extension Services' to mothers, fathers and teachers residing in the surrounding region in order to seek their blessings. The blessings of parents and teachers will bring showers of divine blessings upon TSM and upon the members of DRV, TAP, & TYS.

    (NB: This activity of extending loving and grateful service to parents and teachers is inspired by the ancient Indian dicta *'Matha Pitha Guru Daivom'* (mother, father, and teacher are gods) and *'Mathrudevo Bhava, Pithrudevo Bhava, Acharyadevo Bhava'* (Treat mother, father, and teacher like gods). These dicta call upon us to treat our parents and teachers as representatives of God on earth and serve them with love, gratitude and devotion to receive showers of divine blessings upon us, our families, our communities, and our activities. The moral and spiritual caliber of an individual or a society can be measured in terms of the love, gratitude, and respect shown towards parents and teachers and the selfless service rendered to them by that individual and society. A family or a society that does not respect and serve the parents and teachers with love, respect, and gratitude will fall into moral decay and spiritual apathy sooner or later. India and many other countries in the world today are fast approaching a very dangerous level of moral decay and spiritual apathy. This dangerous situation can be overcome only with divine grace. Hence, seeking the much-needed divine grace through the blessings of parents and teachers by serving them with love and devotion is an urgent and very important task of the era (*Yuga Dharma*) ahead of us today.

2. To serve as autonomous 'Dharma Bharathi Institutes of Peace & Value Education' (DBIs) affiliated to DBNI-Lucknow for promoting a culture of love, peace, and sustainable development through communal harmony, interreligious understanding and national integration based on the Fundamental Duties of Indian citizens given under Article: 51-A of the Indian Constitution & appropriate Constituents of the *Dharma Bharathi Darsana Samhita*. This will provide a very strong interreligious and Constitutional foundation for TSM.

    (NB: Responsible citizenship is the basis of nation-building. The Indian society with its centuries-long 'subject mentality' very urgently needs today a responsible citizenship consciousness through which 'We, the People of India', especially the youth of India, can be motivated to think more about their duties and responsibilities than about their rights and privileges. Printing and distributing the Fundamental Duties at cost price will be part of this activity.)

3. To serve as 'Centers of Inner Peace Meditation' by promoting the 'Shanti Yajna Meditation' - a meditation for inner peace through the Christ-Spirit of forgiveness and reconciliation. 'Shanti Yajna Meditation' is the 'Common Basic Programme' of TSM (Ref. chapter-2 of the mission manual of TSM & Constituent-11 of Part-Two of this book for details of 'Shanti Yajna Meditation'). *Christusishya Shanti Sangham* (Chapter-3) will be responsible for teaching and promoting the 'Shanti Yajna Meditation'.

4. To serve as 'Mothers' Houses' (*Mathru Bhavans*) that will serve nourishing vegetarian food to needy people, especially to senior citizens and children in the region, using the products of the organic farming done by members of DRV, TAP & TYS in the

lands made available to them for this purpose by members of TMS, TPS, & TGS under the *'Tyagarchana Jaiva Samrudhi'* which is the 'Foundational Constructive Programme' of TSM.

5. To serve as 'Training & Coordination Centers' for eco-friendly self-employment initiatives in the Cooperative, Partnership, & Trusteeship Sectors for youth and women based on the eco-spiritual ideology of *Tyagarchana*, and to coordinate their activities under the guidance of Dharma Bharathi Mission (DBM) using its 3-E methodology of 'Education, Employment, and Empowerment'.

C.   Organization of TSM

TSM will be organized in the form of a network of autonomous local 'CESR Communities' under the leadership of TAP and guidance of DRV with the help of DBM. Members of CSS will provide the soul force and inner spiritual dynamism to the CESR Communities of TSM.

A local 'CESR Community' will include the members of TAP, TYS. TMS, TPS, & TGS in that locality.

A 'Tyagarchana Shanti Bhavan' established in the locality will serve as the 'spiritual home' & 'meeting point' for the members of the local CESR Community of TSM.

*   *   *   *   *   *   *   *

The Kerala Pilot Project of TSM

The reoriented TSM was inaugurated by Hon. Justice Kurian Joseph, former Judge of the Supreme Court of India, & Mentor, Dharma Rajya Vedi, during the *'Sarva Dharma Shanti Sangamam'* organized by DRV on 10 & 11 December 2021 at YMCA, Aluva. A 20-year pilot project to transform Kerala into an inspirational role model for a culture of love, peace, and sustainable development in the world was also envisaged in this '*Sarva Dharma Shanti Sangamam*'.

'*Chaitanya Kerala Mahayajnam*' is the name chosen for the 20-year Kerala pilot project of TSM envisaged in the '*Sarva Dharma Shanti Sangamam*'. This name was chosen unanimously by the 10 members of TAP who successfully completed the first Foundation Course of the Master Trainers Training Programme (MTTP) organized by DRV in Dharma Bharathi Ashram from 05 February to 05 March 2022 in collaboration with Navasrushti Academy of Integral Leadership (NAIL).

The MTTP was conducted based on the mission manual of TSM that was released and dedicated to God and humanity in Dharma Bharathi Ashram on 30 January 2022, the 74th anniversary of the martyrdom of Mahatma Gandhi.

'*Chaitanya Kerala Mahayajnam*' aims to make Kerala an inspirational role model of a culture of love, peace, and sustainable development in the pandemic-devastated and violence-ridden world based on the vision, ideology, and action plan of TSM under the guidance of DRV and leadership of TAP through a network of CESR Communities & TSBs. TYS will provide the task force for these CESR Communities & TSBs of TSM. DRV will provide the moral support and CSS will provide the soul force for the *Chaitnaya Kerala Mahayajnam*. DBM will provide support for the socio-economic development programmes of this Kerala pilot project.

NIT-Kerala (also termed 'Navasrushti Kerala Mission') will be the legal holder and accounting authority of this historic 20-year Kerala pilot project. DRV through TAP and TYS, and with the support and collaboration of other organizations and institutions functioning under the legal ownership of NIT, will be responsible to promote the *Chaitanya Kerala Mahayajnam* and to achieve its aim and objectives.

The vision, ideology, and action programmes as well as the goal and plan of action of *Chaitanya Kerala Mahayajnam* are briefly outlined below for ready reference.

1.   The Vision of *Chaitanya Kerala Mahayajnam*

The inclusive vision of a greater India adopted and promoted by DRV for the '*Chaitanya Kerala Mahayajnam*' is that of a spiritually awakened, morally regenerated, economically prosperous and politically strong '*Bharatiya Dharma Rajya*'. This vision of a greater India is based on the Fundamental Duties of Indian Citizens (*Bharatiya Dharma*) given under Article 51-A of the Indian Constitution.

India is a large 'Joint Family' of many cultures, religions, languages, and ethnicities. 'We, the People of India' are members of this large Joint Family. We are also responsible citizens of the Sovereign Democratic Republic of India, and hence are called to live in harmony with one another.

The '*Bharatiya Dharma Rajya*' of our vision will be a land and light of love, peace, and sustainable development in the pandemic-devastated and violence-ridden world. She will be a mother of love and princess of peace in the world family of nations, and a disciple nation of God on earth.

The Kerala prototype of *Bharatiya Dharma Rajya* is termed '*Chaitanya Keralam*'. It is the inclusive vision of a great new Kerala adopted and promoted by DRV for the *Chaitanya Kerala Mahayajnam*.

Chaitanya Keralam will be a land of '*one caste, one religion, and one God for humankind*' as envisioned by Sri Narayana Guru, and a land of the *'Gram Swaraj'* as envisioned by Mahatma Gandhi. In the context of TSM, the one caste that is being presented and promoted by DRV is 'Sacrifice'/ *Tyagam*; the one religion is 'Service'/ *Sevanam*, and the one God is 'Love'/*Sneham*.

The *'Gram Swaraj'* vision of Mahatma Gandhi can be realized in Kerala, when the Panchayati Raj Act 1992 is put into practice fully, both in letter and spirit, in the State beyond the divisive party politics and self-destructive corruption, casteism, and communalism.

'Chaitanya Keralam' will have an *Islamic body* of prayerfulness and fellowship; a *Hindu mind* of *nishkama karma* and earth-family consciousness; and a *Christian heart* of self-sacrificing love and selfless service. This vision of *Chaitanya Keralam* is also the vision of a spiritually awakened, morally regenerated, economically prosperous, and politically strong great new Kerala built on the strong foundation of the Fundamental Duties of Indian citizens (*Bharatiya Dharma*), and inspired by the divine values of *sneham, tyagam & sevanam* (love, sacrifice, and service).

Bharatiya Dharma Rajya & Chaitanya Keralam will constitute the inclusive interreligious and eco-spiritual visions that are being presented and promoted by DRV for the *Chaitanya Kerala Mahayajnam*. The global vision will be that of an Earth Family ('*Vasudhaivakutumbakam*').

2.   The Ideology of *Chaitanya Kerala Mahayajnam*

The ideology adopted and promoted by DRV for *Chaitanya Kerala Mahayajnam* is the eco-spiritual ideology of *'Tyagarchana'*. This eco-spiritual ideology is presented in detail under Constituent-8 in Part-Two of this book. *Tyagarchana* is also explained in chapter-4b of the book 'Integral Renaissance of India' and in chapter-3B of the mission manual of TSM.

3.   Action Programmes of *Chaitanya Kerala Mahayajnam*

The 3-tier comprehensive action programmes inspired by the Gandhian model applied effectively for the Freedom Struggle of India is also adopted for the *Chaitanya Kerala Mahayajnam*. The Gandhian model consisted of a Common Basic Programme, 18 Constructive Action Programmes and issue-based and time-bound Liberative Action Campaigns like 'Champaran Satyagraha', 'Kheda Satyagraha', 'Rowlatt Satyagraha', 'Salt Satyagraha' etc.

Following the Gandhian model, DRV has developed and adopted a 3-tier comprehensive action programme for *Chaitanya Kerala Mahayajnam*. This 3-tier comprehensive action programme consists of a Common Basic Programme, five Constructive Action Programmes and a Liberative Action Campaign.

a.   The Common Basic Programme

The 'Common Basic Programme' of *Chaitanya Kerala Mahayajnam* promoted by DRV & TAP is termed *'Tyagarchana Shanti Yajnam'*. This Common Basic Programme involves practicing and promoting the *'Shanti Yajna'* meditation daily for minimum 15 minutes for peace within individuals, families, and communities in Kerala through forgiveness and reconciliation. Peace within individuals and families is the basic requirement for peace in the world. The *'Shanti Yajna'* meditation is presented in Part-Two of this book under Constituent-11, and in chapter-2 of the mission manual of TSM. One needs to practice it daily to develop peace within one's own life and within one's family/ community through forgiveness, reconciliation, gratitude, and self-surrender.

b.   The Five Constructive Action Programmes

Tyagarchana Jaiva Samrudhi, Tyagarchana Pancha Sutra, Tyagarchana Santhushta Kuttikalam, Tyagarchana Purna Swaraj & Tyagarchana Kritajnatha Yajnam constitute the five Constructive

Action Programmes of *Chaitanya Kerala Mahayajnam.* These are briefly explained below:

1. *'Tyagarchana Jaiva Samrudhi'*: This is the Foundational Constructive Programme of *Chaitanya Kerala Mahayajnam.* It involves promoting eco-friendly life style, organic food habits and holistic healthcare systems among the people of Kerala. In simple practical terms, it involves setting apart a minimum amount of Rs. 10/- and one hour of physical labour as *Tyagarchana* every day and using them to produce organic vegetables and fruits for one's own family/community.

2. *'Tyagarchana Pancha Sutra'*: This is the five-point Constructive Action Programme of *Chaitanya Kerala Mahayajnam* for the moral regeneration of Kerala based on *Prarthana Sutra* (Praying daily for peace and happiness according to one's own religious tradition and in one's own time and place), *Padhai Sutra* (Regular study of scriptures of all religions and other inspiring books), *Safai Sutra* (Cleanliness of body, mind, and surroundings), *Seva Sutra* (Service to parents and teachers as well as to the needy fellow human beings) and *Prem Sutra* (Speaking and doing things with love).

3. *'Tyagarchana Santhushta Kuttikalam'*: This is a four-point Constructive Action Programme to promote the health and happiness of all children below 18 years of age in Kerala. It consists of caring love, nutritious food, value education, and playing, singing and dancing.

4. *'Tyagarchana Purna Swaraj'*: This is a Constructive Action Programme for the economic, social, and moral freedoms that are yet to be won for India. Putting into practice the Panchayati Raj Act passed by the Parliament of India in 1992, both in letter and spirit, beyond the sectarian party/ caste/communal

politics is the most important step towards realizing this goal in Kerala.

5. *'Tyagarchana Kritanjatha Yajnam'*: This is a Constructive Action Programme to promote an attitude of gratitude in the hearts and minds of people in Kerala. This is a socio-spiritual programme that involves setting apart at least a few minutes every day morning to thank God for the gift of yet another new day, and at least a few minutes every night before going to bed for thanking God for the many blessings received during the day. We also need to thank our family members, friends, and relatives for the help rendered to us by them and for the good words spoken to/about us by them.

c. The Liberative Action Campaign

The on-going Liberative Action Campaign adopted and promoted by DRV for *Chaitanya Kerala Mahayajnam* is termed *'Paura Dharma Mahayajnam'* (also known as *'Tyagarchana Paura Dharmam'*). This is an Interreligious Campaign to liberate the people of Kerala from their 'subject mentality' by promoting the Fundamental Duties of Indian citizens (*Bharatiya Dharma*) given under Article: 51-A of the Indian Constitution as a Peace & Value Education project to develop 'responsible citizenship consciousness' among people of Kerala, more so among teachers and students in Kerala.

4. The Goal of *Chaitanya Kerala Mahayajnam*

The goal of *Chaitanya Kerala Mahayajnam* is to make Kerala an inspirational role model of love, peace, and sustainable development in the pandemic-devastated and violence-ridden world through interreligious cooperative action based on its vision, ideology, and action plan of TSM presented above.

5.   **The Plan of Action for *Chaitanya Kerala Mahayajnam***

The goal of *Chaitanya Kerala Mahayajnam* will be achieved inter alia through the following plan of action:

1. DRV & TAP will promote communal harmony and interreligious cooperation for a culture of love, peace, and sustainable development in Kerala by undertaking *Sarva Dharma Tyagarchana Shanti Yatras* (Travels/ Tours across the State to promote communal harmony and interreligious cooperation based on the vision, ideology, and action plan of TSM), by organizing *Sarva Dharma Tyagarchana Shanti Sangamams* (Public Meetings to promote communal harmony and interreligious cooperation based on the vision, ideology, and action plan of TSM) and by conducting *Sarva Dharma Tyagarchana Prarthana Yajnams* (Meditation & Prayer sessions/ programmes to promote communal harmony and interreligious cooperation based on the vision, ideology, and action plan of TSM). Without communal harmony and interreligious cooperation, the *Chaitanya Kerala Mahayajnam* cannot succeed in ushering in a culture of love, peace, and sustainable development in this State. The first two years (2022 - 2023) are to be devoted mainly for this most important task of developing communal harmony and interreligious cooperation in Kerala.

2. DRV & TAP will educate the people of Kerala, especially the students and teachers in Kerala, on the vision, ideology, and action plan of TSM as well as on the Enlightened Leadership Principles and Mission Methodologies of TSM by organizing and conducting study classes, workshops, seminars etc. at different places, especially in High Schools, Colleges and Universities, in Kerala in collaboration with like-minded organizations and institutions. Students and teachers will be encouraged and motivated to form TYS and TGS units in

their Schools/Colleges/Universities for promoting the vision, ideology and action plan of TSM in order to usher in a culture of love, peace, and sustainable development in Kerala.

3. DRV & TAP will select, train and motivate talented members to form Cultural Troupes/ Literary Clubs/ Legal Cells/ Media Cells etc., and to serve as Spokespersons/ Resource Persons etc. for the purpose of educating, inspiring and motivating the people of Kerala, especially the youth and students in the State, to understand and make their own the vision, ideology and action plan of TSM.

4. DRV & TAP will establish Local Units of TYS at different places and in Schools, Colleges & Universities in Kerala to achieve the aim of *Chaitanya Kerala Mahayajnam*. DRV & TAP will also establish a network of TSBs in Kerala as training and coordination centers for members of TYS and as rehabilitation centers for like-minded & needy TMS/TPS/TGS members.

5. Training & orientation programmes in enlightened leadership, entrepreneurship, development, & skill development will be organized by DRV & TAP for members of TYS in collaboration with other like-minded Institutions/ Organizations.

6. Trained members of TYS will be motivated to undertake a membership-drive for TMS, TPS, & TGS in their locality. They will extend loving care to the members of TMS, TPS, and TGS in their area of operation so that these mothers, fathers, and teachers will never be left alone and unloved. Members of TYS can begin their mission by establishing a 'help-line' or 'call center' for members of TMS/TPS/TGS to contact them whenever needed.

7. Well-trained members of TYS will be encouraged and motivated to launch various Cooperative/ Partnership/ Trusteeship socio-

economic initiatives for sustainable development of Kerala and for making themselves and their TSBs economically self-supporting through their own initiatives with the blessings and the emotional and financial support of the members of TMS, TPS, & TGS and of the members of DRV & TAP.

8. Well-trained members of TYS will be enabled and guided by DRV & TAP to promote a truly decentralized, value-based and spiritualized democracy based on the Fundamental Duties of Indian citizens enshrined under Article: 51-A of the Indian Constitution, and on the Panchayati Raj Act passed and adopted by the Parliament of India in 1992.

9. After becoming economically self-supporting through their own initiatives, the members of TYS will be encouraged to work as 'Missionaries of TSM' for promoting a culture of love, peace, and sustainable development in Kerala.

10. The 'Missionaries of TSM' will promote a spiritualized, decentralized and value-based political system, and a spiritualized, decentralized and value-based economic order for abiding peace and sustainable development in Kerala. They will work tirelessly, fearlessly, and prayerfully for making the State an inspirational role model of the much-needed spiritualization of economics and politics through interreligious cooperative action based on the vision, ideology and action plan of TSM.

*   *   *   *   *   *   *   *

The Tyagarchana Shanti Mission and its Kerala pilot project are inspired by the living Spirit of Christ. These are interreligious and eco-spiritual initiatives for giving practical expressions to the 'Indian face of the Christian faith' presented in Part-Two of this book without religious conversion and cultural alienation.

Kerala is the cradle of the Christian faith in India. But unfortunately, many of the Churches in Kerala today are being enslaved by an all pervasive moral decay and spiritual apathy. Some of them have been wasting their energies and resources on issues of power, property, and liturgy which have very little relevance to the real spirit of Christian faith.

A return to the living Spirit of Christ and the 'cross' of Christ is the only way to save Kerala and the pandemic-devastated world. The Tyagarchana Shanti Mission and its Kerala pilot project are creative responses to this call of history and destiny.

Appendix A

In Search of the Common Aspects in Christianity and Hinduism

Introduction

The first official declaration of the Christian Church regarding the necessity of conducting dialogue with other religions in the world was perhaps made by the II Vatican Council in 1965 in its famous declaration called Nostra Acetate. It was really a positive statement of the Roman Catholic Church about the religions of the world. The World Council of Churches (WCC) was rather slow in making a statement regarding the relation of the Christian Churches with other religions.

About one and a half decade later, that means in 1979, the WCC adopted a set of "Guidelines on Dialogue". In these Guidelines the neighbours or believers in other religions were regarded not as outsiders, but as 'fellow-pilgrims' in our journey to eternal salvation.

When we think of the presence of the Christians in India, one truth is hidden to majority of the Hindu brothers and sisters: the truth that the Christian faith came to India in the 1st century itself. Majority of the people in India have a misunderstanding that the Christian faith was imported to India by the Christian missionaries from western Europe when the Europeans came to colonize India in later middle age.

The Christian faith in Western Europe has an average of only 1500 years of history but the Christian faith in India, particularly in Kerala, has 2000 years of history. The Hindus and Christians were living together in Kerala as brothers and sisters in total harmony and co-operation and helping each other. As far as I know, in ancient times the Christian Churches were constructed in the form of Hindu Temples or Ambalams. The Church Architecture was totally changed after the coming of the Portuguese in late Middle Ages and the present western style was adopted and accepted only later. In AD 52 St. Thomas the Apostle came to India not to introduce a new religion, but to introduce a new *way of life* taught by Jesus Christ. In Indian terminology we call it 'Christu Marga'.

The Christu Marga is the way of self-sacrificing love, the way of humility, the way of service, peace and reconciliation. Jesus Christ announced the Kingdom of God in which God is presented as the loving and caring Father in Heaven, and thus the human race becomes His sons and daughters, thus realizing the universal brotherhood of the human race. In no way Christu Marga brings out conflict, quarrel, disharmony and enmity. On the contrary, it brings out self-sacrificing love, peace, co-operation and reconciliation. Jesus Christ as Son of God showed in his own life an eternal and everlasting model for the life of the sons and daughters in the Kingdom of God. The final aim of the Hindu spiritual teachings is to establish 'Dharma Rajya'. 'Dharma Rajya' in Hinduism can be compared to the Kingdom of God in the New Testament. According to Bhagavat Gita the incarnation of God takes place from time to time to abolish evil and to establish

Dharma and Dharma Rajya. Let us now examine the similarities in the teachings of Hinduism and Christianity.

1.   The Concept of *OM* in Hinduism and *Logos* in the Bible

OM is the most important symbol used in Hinduism. In front of the Hindu temples and institutions we can see this symbol either written or inscribed. We have to grasp the deep theological implications of this symbol. In Sanskrit language 'A' is the first letter of the alphabet and 'M' is the last syllable. In English 'A' is the first letter and 'Z' is the last letter. 'A & Z' in English means everything from A to Z. It represents the totality of something. Similarly, OM represents everything from the beginning to the end. A similar expression is found in the Bible and it is called Alpha and Omega (Rev 1:8). Alpha is the first letter and Omega is the last letter in the Greek language. The dictionary meaning of the expression Alpha and Omega is beginning and the end. In Hinduism OM is the Symbol for Brahman, and Brahman means God. OM is also the word filled with the power of God. It is considered as the sacred monosyllable. It is the boat to take you to the other shore of fearlessness and immortality. The concept OM is the most important name of Brahman, who is also the Supreme Spirit. According to John 4:24 God is Spirit, and those who worship Him must worship in Spirit and truth.

God is, according to Hinduism, 'Satchidananda'. The word Satchidananda is formed out of three divine existential qualities: 'Sat' means essence, 'Chit' means knowledge and 'Ananda' means bliss or supreme happiness. 'Satchidananda', therefore, means essence absolute, knowledge absolute and bliss absolute. When we hear the sound or symbol OM, it also denotes Satchidananda.

OM is the word uttered and spoken. The whole universe comes out of OM and through OM and absorbed in OM. OM is the Word of God and the Word of God cannot be separated from God and thus OM and Brahman (God) are inseparable. Logos (word) is one of the most important concepts in Greek philosophy and it is equal to God and this concept is used in the beginning of the 4th Gospel to depict Jesus Christ – the Son of God. Logos is, in very simple terms, the Word of God. 'In the beginning was the Logos(=Word) and the Word was with God and the Word was God. He was in the beginning with God; and all things were made through him and without him was not anything made that was made" (Jn. 1:1-3). According to these verses, God created the whole universe through the Word. The same idea is found in the beginning of the Bible in the creation story. Here the creation of the universe takes place through the Word spoken by God (Genesis Chapter 1).

OM contains three divine sounds. They are A, U and M. A represents the beginning or origin, U represents the sustaining and M represents the end. OM in this sense represents the beginning, sustaining and the end of the whole universe.

From the above statements from the Bible, we have seen that the origin of the whole Universe is God. Logos or Word is the mediator and sustainer (Saviour) of the whole creation (universe). Jesus Christ the incarnated Word will come at the end of the ages to judge the final destiny of the whole universe.

Swami Sivananda, one of the famous teachers of Hinduism says: "You will find in the Bible; in the beginning was the Word and the Word was with God and the Word was God. This is OM the word of power...... This word has come out of OM, exists in OM and dissolves in OM. The creation itself is set in motion by the vibration of OM".[1] The word 'Amen' is used in the Bible and used by the Christians at the end of their prayers. Muslims use the word 'Ahmin' during prayers. Amen and Ahmin are simply different forms of OM.

In Hinduism a Teacher or Guru occupies a unique position. To get eternal knowledge and wisdom and for the development of the personality, concentrated learning and hard training under a Guru is necessary. Complete dedication and obedience to Guru is expected. Guru is a person enlightened by God and he is able to utter the Word of God. In this sense OM appears as the voice of the Guru and the disciples of the Guru hear the word of God from the Guru. In this sense according to Sivananda 'OM is Guru's voice'. When Jesus began his public ministry, his main activity was the preaching and teaching the Word of God. When the people approached Jesus, they greeted him calling Guru or teacher. Only a few people recognised him as Son of God, and the common people considered him as a Guru. At least for three years Jesus taught his disciples divine truths and gave them hard training, so that they may become preachers of the Word of God. After the time of Jesus, the disciples became preachers and teachers of the Word of God.

OM as eternal sound and Word of God is also attributed to the begotten Son. The 'son' is begotten out of Golden Egg called Hiranyagerbha. According to Sivananda[2] OM is the voice of Hiranyagerbha and OM is also Akshara Brahman.[3]

---

[1] Swami Sivananda Meditations on OM, Divine Life Society, Himalaya, UP 1941 P.8

[2] Meditations on OM P.16

[3] Akshara means word or Alphabet.

Rohit Mehta,[4] one of the well-known philosophers, expresses his opinion regarding the relation between Word and God in the following words: "The soundless sound is indeed the Naada - Brahma[5] (Naada= sound, Brahman = God).

Not only was the Word with God, the Word was God. The Word being with God, signifies manifestation emanating from God – but the Word being God is the un-manifest state.

What is with a person can be differentiated. But what is a person cannot be differentiated.

According to Swami Prabhavananda[6] OM is the eternal word manifested within the shrine of the heart of Brahman. He says: "once upon a time, before the historic account of man was attempted, Brahman, the first born of God was meditating upon the Supreme Brahman, whom through His Grace there was manifested within the shrine of His heart the eternal Word OM (the Logos), the seed of all knowledge and of all thoughts...." Prabhavananda compares OM with the Logos in the Gospel of John.

2.   The Concept of Aswatha Tree from Heaven in Upanishad

The 6th chapter of Kathopanishad makes the following reference about the Aswatha tree: "This is the ancient Aswatha tree whose roots are above and whose branches are below. That is verily the pure Brahman and that is also called immortal. In that rest all the worlds and none can transcend it. Verily this is that".

The Aswatha tree in Upanishad represents symbolically God himself. Above means heaven and below refers to earth. The

---

[4] Rohit Mehta, The call of the Upanishads (Publ. Motilal Banarsidas) Delhi 1970, P..148.

[5] Naada – Brahma can also be called as Sabda-Brahma.

[6] Swami Prabhavananda, Vedic Religion and Philosophy, Sri Rama Krishna Matt. Madras P. 22.

Aswatha tree is different from all other trees because its roots are up in heaven.   The roots of all other trees are on the contrary on earth. The reference about the Aswatha tree in Upanishad can be compared with the sayings of Jesus about himself in the fourth Gospel. Jesus appears in this world as an ordinary human being. But Jesus explains the great difference between his humanity and that of the ordinary human beings.

In his conversation with unbelieving Jews, Jesus said to them:"You are from below, I am from above. You are of this world; I am not of this world" (Jn 8:23). Jesus is the Aswatha tree came down from heaven to the earth. The tree came down to the earth to give eternal shelter to humankind. The eternal shelter is given through the sacrifice of the Aswatha tree. Its sacrifice is an eternal sacrifice of God.

The sacrifice and cutting of the Aswatha tree can be compared with the reference about Messiah as the suffering servant in Is 53. The coming of the Aswatha tree from heaven to earth can be compared to the coming of Jesus Christ from heaven to earth.

3.   Prajapathy as Incarnation of God

The most striking similarity between Hinduism and Christianity is found in the presentation of the character 'Prajapathy' in Hinduism and Jesus Christ in Christianity. Prajapathy is Saviour and Lord of humankind.

The Vedas as sacred books of Hinduism, represents scholastic Hinduism. The Puranas can be considered as sacred scriptures of popular Hinduism. The Puranas contain dramatic descriptions of God's activities and speaks of 10 incarnations. But the Vedas representing the scholastic Hinduism speak of only one incarnation and that is 'Prajapathy'. Regarding the origin and nature of 'Prajapathy', Koshy Abraham makes a clear statement: "From

Paramatma (eternal spirit), the great glorious Self, Prajapathy is born in the same glorious form as first born before all creatures of the universe. On his birth itself he is ordained as the only protector of all the visible and invisible on earth and in the rest of the universe. That is to say, he is appointed as the HEIR of all things".[7] According to Hebr. 1:2 Jesus Christ is the HEIR of all things" and mediator of the creation. All the qualities of Christ defined in the Nicene creed is found in Prajapathy also.

We can enumerate the following qualities of Prajapathy: "He is the true light from real light and God the Spirit. He is the first born and self-born before all creatures"[8]. He is not only the creator and supporter of everything visible and invisible in the universe, but also the sustainer of all creatures. The past, present, and future of the world is determined by Prajapathy. According to Rigveda 10:90:2. Prajapathy was the creator of the world in the past, protector of the world in the present, and he will be the saviour of the world in future.

Prajapathy is also called Purusha or Man. The incarnation of Purusha is explained in Purushasuktam. According to Purushasuktam 10:90:2 the whole world is filled with Purusha; the past, the present, and the future are also filled with Purusha. He as the Lord of immortality came down transcending the matter. In the Gospels Jesus Christ is pictured as the Son of Man who will come at the end of the ages with power and great glory. In the case of the possession of super natural powers and glory, Purusha in Rigveda and Son of Man in the Gospels are similar characters.[9]

---

[7] Koshy Abraham, Prajapathy, the Cosmic Christ, ISPCK, Delhi 1997, P.13
[8] Koshy Abraham, Prajapathy P.14.
[9] Mt 24: 29-31; Mk 13:24-27; Lk 21: 25-28.

4.   Importance of Yaga or Sacrifice in Hinduism and in the Christian Teaching

Hinduism gives great importance to Yaga and Pooja for the forgiveness of sins and to receive blessings from God. In the course of time, in practice the importance of Yaga and Pooja was perhaps over emphasized for material benefits, and the priestly class began to exploit the common people imposing on them to bear the costly expenses of Yagas and Poojas. It is believed that Buddhism emerged as a protest against such a development in Hinduism. The concept of yaga or sacrifice is very important in the Old Testament and the New Testament. According to the New Testament, Jesus Christ sacrificed his own life for the salvation of the human race. The death of Jesus on the cross is a Yaga. In the same sense Purusha or Prajapathy is considered as the sacrifical victim for the salvation of the humankind. Yaga is closely related to Tyaga and Tyaga means self-sacrifice. Prajapathy and Jesus Christ are embodiments of Yaga and Tyaga and these two divine qualities were put into practice for the salvation of the human race.   Let us examine some of the similarities in the case of the sacrificial victims Prajapathy and Jesus Christ. Both sacrificed their lives for the salvation of the human race. We can point out the following similarities in the case of the two sacrificial victims.

    a.   The sacrificial man has to be separated from others.[10]

    b.   The sacrificial man should be a silent sufferer.[11]

    c.   He seeks neither release nor turning back.

    d.   The sacrificial animal should be closely tied to the wooden pillar.[12] Jesus was the sacrificial lamb nailed to the wooden cross.[13]

---

[10] Sathpatha Brahmana 13:6:2:2; Mt 2:27-28.
[11] Rigveda 5:46:1; Is 53:7; Mt 27:14.
[12] Sathpatha Brahman 3:7:3.
[13] Brahadaranyaka Upanishad.

e. The blood of the sacrificial man should be shed for the forgiveness sins.[14]

f. The bones of the sacrificial man should not be broken.[15] When Jesus was crucified on the cross the soldiers came to break the legs but didn't do that. But one of the soldiers pierced his side with a spear and at once ·there came out blood and water.[16]

g. The sacrificial victim should return to life after the sacrifice.[17] Jesus was crucified and he died on the cross and was buried. But he resurrected on the third day and returned to life.

Let us now examine the sum and substance of the divine ways revealed to humanity by Jesus Christ and Prajapathy. The two characters - Jesus Christ in Christianity and Prajapathy in Hinduism - reveal similar divine way for human salvation and for Universal peace and unity of mankind. According to scholastic Hinduism and as per the teachings of Jesus Christ the divine ways for the salvation and unity of the human race and for universal peace are the way of self-sacrifice and the way of self-denial. Self-sacrifice is practiced aiming at the welfare of the fellow human beings and in the same way self- denial is practiced to fulfill the needs of the fellow human beings. But unfortunately, the majority of the people in this world are adopting or forced to adopt the satanic ways in their lives to fulfill their selfish needs and to achieve happiness. The satanic ways are just opposite to the above mentioned divine ways. Instead of self-sacrifice, the way of selfishness is adopted.

---

[14] "....... without shedding of the blood there is no forgiveness of sins (Hebr 9:22)

[15] Aitareya Brahmana 2:6 prescribes that the sacrificer should separate the 26 ribs of the animal carefully without breaking them.

[16] John 19:36-37. Here the OT prophecies in Ex 12:46 and Zach 12:10 were fulfilled.

[17] Brahadarnyaaka Upanishad 3:9:28:4-5

Selfishness in essence is denial and ignoring of the fellow human beings. In the satanic way, instead of self-denial, self-assertion is adopted and practiced. Self-assertion is in essence denial and suppression of the fellow human beings and their welfare. Yaga and Tyaga are in separable divine concepts for human peace and unity. On the earth 7.9 billion or 790 crores of people are living and so extensive is the size of the population. If the people on earth adopt the divine ways in their lives, the Kingdom of God and the universal peace can be realized. If the people on earth adopt the satanic ways, then the world will become a place of conflicts, quarrels, and decline.

5.   Incarnation in Popular Hinduism

The technical terminology used in Hinduism for incarnation is Avatar. The Holy Scripture of Popular Hinduism is called Puranas. Contrary to Scholastic Hinduism, the Puranas and the popular Hinduism speak of ten Avatars.

They are:

1.	Malsyaha	–	fish
2.	Kukmaha	-	Tortoise
3.	Varaha	-	Swine
4.	Narasimha	-	Half man and half lion
5.	Vamana	-	Boy
6.	Parasurama	-	youth
7.	Balarama	-	Housefather
8.	Sri-Rama	-	Man of meditation
9.	Sri-Krishna	-	Perfect man
10.	Kalki	-	Judgement & destruction

There are different interpretations regarding the ten avatars or incarnations. According to some scholars, the ten Avatars denote the ten stages in the development and formation of man. According to some others, they are the different ages in the history of humanity.

The last Avatar or incarnation is called 'Kalki' and the details regarding this incarnation is dealt with in Kalki-purana. Kalki-purana deals with the last age and the end time. The eschatological end time is called Kali-kala or Kaliyugam. Kali-kala is the age of judgement and destruction. Kali is the embodiment of all evil (Atharmamurthy).

At the end of the ages the whole world will be filled with all sorts of evil and Kali, which is called Atharmamurthy or devil, will try to establish his Kingdom. But then Kalki will appear to destroy Kali. The age of Kalki will be an age of judgment and destruction. Kalki will destroy the wicked and bring the righteous to Vishnulokam, which means heaven. The coming of Kalki at the end of the ages can be compared to the coming of the Son of Man to judge the world and human race. "When the Son of Man comes in his glory, and all the angels with him, then he will sit on the throne of his glory. All the nations will be gathered before him and he will separate people one from one another ..... The wicked will get eternal punishment and the righteous eternal life."[18]

6.   Bhagavat Gita on Incarnation

Bhagavat Gita, one of the Holy Scriptures of Hindus, is considered as the New Testament of Hinduism. The statement made in Bhagavat Gita regarding the purpose of incarnation is well known to almost all the Hindus. Incarnation takes place from time to time to prevent the Adharma or evil and to re-establish Dharma or justice. The following passage in Bhagavat Gita is well-known to the majority of the people:

---

[18] Mt 25: 31-46.

"Yatha Yathathi Dharmasya Glanirbavathi Bharatha

Abhyathanam Adharmasya Thadatmanam Srujamahyam

Parithranaya Sadhunam Vinasaya Chathushkkratham

Dharma Samsthapanarthaya Sambhavami YugeYuge" (BG 4: 7)

The purpose of the incarnation of the Son of God Jesus Christ was also to establish Justice and to save the human race from peril. For that he tried to establish the Kingdom of God inviting the people to the Kingdom of God through repentance of their sins.[19] To establish the Kingdom of God, the life of the perfect man Jesus Christ is the perfect and unique model for the human race. His model is self-emptying of one's own glories for the glory of fellow human beings and practicing of self-sacrificing love for the salvation of fellow human beings. Selfishness is the most dangerous and devilish power that binds and enslaves every human being. Everyone, therefore, has to free oneself from this slavery and dedicate his life for the service of God and for the service of fellow human beings. Jesus Christ is the best model to achieve such a way of life and in Indian terminology we call this as Christu Marga.

7.   The Challenging Question to the Christian Churches

If a God-fearing Hindu wanted to follow Jesus Christ and would like to become a member of the Christian Church, then in which Church he will be able to take membership? Before him there are several Churches, which are ready to accept him – the Roman Catholic Church, the Syrian Orthodox Church, the Marthoman Syrian Church, the Church of South India etc. The liturgical traditions and way of worship of all these Churches are also different. The Hindu who wanted to become a follower of Christ and member of the Church will be in total confusion and chaos.

---

[19] "The time is fulfilled and the Kingdom of God has come near; repent and believe in the Gospel" (Mk 1:15)

In such a complex situation what is important? Following the way of Jesus Christ, or conversion and getting membership to a particular Church?

During the last two thousand years Jesus Christ was presented, understood and worshipped according to Syrian, Latin, Byzantine, Armenian, Coptic and in many other traditions. If it is so, why not we present and understand Jesus Christ according to the Indian way of thinking and why not we worship him according to Indian way of worship using familiar Indian terminologies?

The contribution of the Christian Church to humanity is immensely great and nobody can deny this truth. But at the same time in the course of history the Christian Churches were institutionalized and became an oppressive and suppressive body aiming mainly at worldly pomp and pleasure, and at selfish motives, material achievements and benefits. What is essentially needed and expected from Christian Churches is imparting of the Spirit of Christ to humanity. The Spirit of Christ means the spirit of self-sacrificing love, the spirit of self-emptying humility and the spirit of selfless service, which were realized in the person and work of Jesus Christ. We call it 'Christu Marga'. Any deviation from Christu Marga will never lead to reconciliation, peace, sustainable development and unity of humanity.

Conclusion

In Kerala, in South India, for the last 2000 years Hindus and Christians were living together peacefully. Believers in both religions respected each other and never tried to dominate over the other. We can say there was wonderful co-existence, harmony, and co-operation. But one danger that we can smell now is the evil intention to politicize Hinduism and to convert India into a Hindu religious state instead of being a welfare state or Dharma Rajya.

Christianity is here in India from the 1stcentury AD onwards and it is deep-rooted in the Indian soil. The misunderstanding that Christianity is imported from outside must be corrected. For the original Christians in India, their motherland is India and their love for their motherland is so deep in their hearts. In India Hindus and Christians are fellow-pilgrims in their journey to eternal life. But to live together peacefully, we must know each other and understand each other.

NB: I am very glad that Acharyasri has found this Article useful in the mission of promoting the 'Indian face of the Christian faith' in the multi-religious context of India today. I feel that Christianity and Hinduism are natural spiritual allies. Their spiritual communion can give birth to an Integral Renaissance of India as well as to an Integrated World Order. As a close friend and fellow worker of Acharyasri, and as the National Vice President of Dharma Rajya Vedi, I am also fully committed to the mission of promoting the 'Indian face of the Christian faith' without religious conversion and cultural alienation.

- Rev. Dr. Adai Jacob Cor Episcopa
- Founder Principal, Malankara Syrian Orthodox Theological
Seminary & National Vice President, Dharma Rajya Vedi.

Appendix B

Viswa Shanti Peetam

'Viswa Shanti Peetam' (VSP) is envisaged to be a World Peace Center to be established at a suitable location in India, preferably in Kerala, to promote a culture of love, peace, and sustainable development in the pandemic-devastated and violence-ridden world based on the 'Dharma Bharathi' school of thought.

'Peace' is the crying need of the era. There is very little peace in the world today. With the unprecedented agony, pain, suffering, death and devastation caused by COVID-19 pandemic, and with the growing violence and conflicts among communities and nations in the world, the hunger and thirst for peace have increased in geometric proportions. Without lasting peace there can be no holistic health, sustainable development, and abiding happiness for humankind.

Peace and sustainable development in the world are also impossible without interreligious harmony and cooperation. It was perhaps this realization that had motivated the United Nations to organize the *'Millennium World Peace Summit of Religious and Spiritual Leaders'* in New York in August 2000. This was the first World Peace Summit of its kind organized by the United Nations. The most important achievement of this Millennium World Peace

Summit was the signing of a 'Commitment to Global Peace' by the religious and spiritual leaders of the world gathered at the UN for this Summit.

The author of this book was one of the delegates invited from India by the UN for the Millennium World Peace Summit. He represented 'Dharma Rajya Vedi' (DRV) & 'Disciples of Christ for Peace' (DCP). He was also a signatory to the 'Commitment to Global Peace' for and on behalf of DRV & DCP.

The 'Commitment to Global Peace' is included under chapter-2 of the Part-Three of our book. It will serve as the 'inspirational document' for the proposed Viswa Shanti Peetam.

This 'Commitment to Global Peace' has become more relevant in the context of the present pandemic-devastated and violence-ridden world than ever before. Hence, the proposed 'Viswa Shanti Peetam' will strive incessantly and prayerfully to implement the 11-point Plan of Action adopted by the religious and spiritual leaders of the world included in the 'Commitment to Global Peace'. This purpose will be achieved through the 'Dharma Bharathi' school of thought with the power and wisdom of God ever active in human history in, with, and through the living Spirit of Christ.

A book titled 'Viswa Shanti Peetam' authored by me was released by Sri. Arif Mohammad Khan, the Hon. Governor of Kerala, on 14 October 2021 at Gandhi Park, Thiruvananthapuram, Kerala. Some Comments on that book by prominent people are included below.

Comments on 'Viswa Shanti Peetam'

"Millennium World Peace Summit of Religious and Spiritual Leaders organized by the United Nations in August 2000 was a historic event in which my predecessor, the late lamented Dr. Joseph Mar Thoma Metropolitan had participated. He was also a signatory to

the'Commitment to Global Peace' signed at the UN by the religious and spiritual leaders of the world in this Millennium World Peace Summit. In accordance with that document a Centre for World Peace under the name 'Viswa Shanti Peetam' is being initiated in Kerala by Dharma Rajya Vedi to give visible expressions to the contents of the 'Commitment to Global Peace' and to hold Ecumenical and Interreligious Parliaments and Conventions.

I offer my prayerful blessings to this laudable initiative being taken up by Dharma Rajya Vedi under the leadership of Acharyasri Dr. Sachidananda Bharathi, who was also a delegate from India for the Millennium World Peace Summit and a signatory to the 'Commitment to Global Peace'.

India is a land of Peace (Shanti). It has religious and secular connotations. In the midst of conflicts, pandemic, devastations and divisions, the people of India look forward to the establishment of Peace and Harmony. Towards this end, may the Viswa Shanti Peetam prove to be leading the people to progress and to the establishment of the 'Kingdom of God' ('Dharma Rajya') of love, unity, peace, and joy on earth".

Dr. Theodosius Mar Thoma Metropolitan,
Poolatheen,
Tiruvalla - 689 101, Kerala, India.

"We are living in a time of troubles afflicting humanity in many ways. Obviously, those who want to take humanity out of the troubles and towards peace, sanity, and spirituality should get together, ignoring all other differences among themselves, and for that noble purpose the Viswa Shanti Peetam is necessary."

Ambassador K P Fabian IFS (Rtd)
Former Ambassador of India to Italy &National President, DRV
& Professor, Symbiosis University, Pune

"The vision of 'Viswa Shanti Peetam' presented by Swamiji in this book is indeed very inspiring. It is also a dream that many of us have been carrying in our own hearts.

May this shared vision and dream be realized at the earliest by the grace of God and with the generous 'Tyagarchana' of all peace-loving people of goodwill in the pandemic-devastated world. In the present day world, the recognition of plurality as the will of God and the willingness to overcome the dangers of exclusivism, inclusivism and relativism are not only a theological necessity, but also an existential need.

I offer my prayerful blessings and wholehearted support to this World Peace Center and the various establishments envisaged within it."

Dr. Kuriakose Mor Theophilose Metropolitan
President, Ecumenical Commission, Malankara Jacobite Syrian
Orthodox Church, Metropolitan and Professor, MSOTS

"Peace is the crying need of the era. People all over the world hunger and thirst for peace. With the pain, agony, death, and devastation caused by the COVID-19 pandemic, the hunger and thirst for peace are felt more acutely for peace all over the world. The proposed Viswa Shanti Peetam will be a God-sent blessing for humanity at this time.

I offer my best wishes, and pray for abundant divine blessings for its time-bound realization. I would like to compliment Swamiji for this unique and noble idea of establishing the Viswa Shanti Peetam in Kerala as a Universal Center for promoting human brotherhood, ecumenical and interreligious harmony, and unitive spiritual consciousness. This Center will be a World Platform for addressing the moral, spiritual, religious, and cultural issues facing the world. It will be a torch-bearer to universal peace and brotherhood."

Lt. Gen. Ashok Vasudeva, PVSM, AVSM, VSM (Rtd)
National President, Military Christian Fellowship

"The 'Viswa Shanti Peetam' presents a collective vision and mission for the whole humanity. We should all join hands in the mission of promoting viswa shanti, world peace. 'Blessed are the peacemakers, they shall be called the children of God', taught Lord Jesus Christ.

I wish and pray for abundant divine blessings upon the Viswa Shanti Peetam project. I offer my wholehearted support to this International Center."

Justice Kurian Joseph
Former Judge, Supreme Court of India

"The roadmap of Swami Sachidananda Bharathi's Viswa Shanti Peetam as spelt out in this book is indeed brilliant, inspiring and

promising. I wish him good luck and divine blessings in this formidable mission."

Prof. Tahir Mahmood
Former Chairman, National Commission for Minorities
& Vice Chairman, NCRLM & Law Commission of India

"In today's strife torn world, attainment of world peace is the most effective way to put an end to human suffering and save the humongous economic costs of conflicts and their aftermath. World peace is the concept of an ideal state of happiness, freedom and peace within and among all people and nations on planet earth. Establishing the 'Viswa Shanti Peetam' in Kerala is indeed a very noble and lofty vision in the service and for the love of mankind. Viswa Shanti Peetam will be the "fountain of world peace in God's own country". My best wishes for the success of this great vision and project".

Air Marshal Naresh Verma, AVSM, VSM (Rtd)
Former Director General of Administration, Indian Air Force

"The vision of Acharyasri Dr. Sachidananda Bharathi to establish a Viswa Shanti Peetam which implies an International Center for promoting human solidarity, holistic development and integral peace is inspired and motivated by Sadguru Jesus Christ. It is in line with the will of God to establish His Kingdom of love, righteousness, peace and reconciliation on earth.

In the Kingdom of God, the universal brotherhood of the human race will be established. The guiding principles of the Kingdom of God will be selfless love, peace, righteousness, mercy, reconciliation and self-sacrifice.

Let us all pray, do our best and work hard to establish the Viswa Shanti Peetam as early as possible in order to establish the Dharma Rajya, the Kingdom of God, on earth."

Rev. Dr. Adai Jacob Cor-Episcopa
Founder Principal, MSOTS

"The 'Viswa Shanti Peetam' is a great and challenging project. But nothing is impossible for us, if it is done with love for the glory of God and good of humanity. In the present context of the pandemic-devastated world such an International Center to promote human solidarity, holistic development and integral peace, and to house a Global Ecumenical Parliament as well as a Global Interreligious Parliament is also very necessary. I offer my prayerful best wishes for the realization of this inspiring global project. We, the people of Kerala can be proud of such a World Peace Center in our God's own country."

Rt. Rev. Dr. Abraham Mar Paulos Episcopa
Malankara Marthoma Syrian Church, Adoor Diocese

"Kerala is the cradle of Christianity in the Indian Subcontinent. The various Christian Churches have their strong presence in Kerala. The 'Viswa Shanti Peetam' is the vision of an International Center for human solidarity, holistic development and integral peace to be established in Kerala in which all Christian Churches can be partners. I offer my prayerful best wishes to this first CSSR project."

Most Rev. Sylvester Ponnumuthan
Bishop of Punalur
Chairman, KCBC Commission for Ecumenism & Dialogue